Small-Rural Community Colleges

Ministry of Education & Training
MET Library
13th Floor, Mowat Block, Queen's Park
Toronto M7A 1L2

REPORT OF THE
COMMISSION ON
SMALL AND/OR RURAL
COMMUNITY COLLEGES

American Association of Community and Junior Colleges
National Center for Higher Education
Suite 410, One Dupont Circle, NW
Washington, D.C. 20036
(202) 293-7050

Copyright © 1988
Printed in the United States of America
ISBN 0-87117-177-5

INTRODUCTION

For decades there has been a quiet but significant phenomenon occurring in the small and rural communities of America. It has taken place through the evolution of the more than six hundred small community, technical, and junior colleges strategically located throughout the rural communities of America. These colleges frequently represent the only focal point in their respective communities, where a wide range of ideas and problems can be discussed and molded into alternative solutions. There is a sense of neutrality that exists on these campuses that provides the background against which all issues and perspectives can be examined. Frequently these colleges provide the only forum for addressing issues ranging from economic development to the cultural arts.

Although a significant number of students enrolled in the nation's two-year colleges are attending small and rural colleges, there is a dearth of information about the qualities that make these situations somewhat different from their larger urban counterparts. Frequently the research and resulting literature focus on larger, more financially developed systems that are on the cutting edge of innovation.

The American Association of Community and Junior Colleges (AACJC) Commission on Small/Rural Community Colleges has therefore set about preparing this monograph to help create a basis of information from which we hope additional research will be stimulated.

We have determined that the issues and problems for the small and rural college are essentially the same as those of our larger urban counterparts. What is different, however, is the method of responding to the issues or solving the problems. In almost all cases the small/rural college must be extremely comprehensive in its interpretation of community services and curriculum. For example, in communities where there may not be an arts council, a theater within which to perform, or a museum, or other culturally related facilities or organizations, the local community college might be called upon to provide all of these components and to provide the leadership to manage them. All this is done without additional funds and frequently without the support of a large college foundation. In most cases the results will not stand out as national models but may very well represent the total cultural initiative available to thousands of people. The same examples can be drawn in other areas such as economic development.

To identify some of the unique approaches used by small and rural colleges, the commission surveyed nearly six hundred institutions in the 1986/87 academic year. The following chapters, written by commission members, represent a synthesis of data.

                                          D. Kent Sharples
                                        President
                                        Horry-Georgetown Technical College

TWO-YEAR COLLEGE EDUCATION ON THE HORIZON

By Gerald Fisher

As the last decade of the twentieth century approaches, the United States finds itself in a period of painful self-examination. To put it simply, many things are not going well for us. We have not solved the internal social and educational problems that we attacked so vigorously and optimistically in the 1960s. We continue to fret about many aspects of our international leadership role, and, to our great surprise and chagrin, our national economic base and standard of living have been eroding steadily for a number of years.

All of this would have been unimaginable to most Americans at the end of World War II. We had emerged from that conflict as the richest and most powerful of nations. We accepted this role seriously—perhaps too seriously—and proceeded with the task of helping both former allies and enemies in peacetime rebuilding, although there were those who scoffed at our efforts and said that as a people we were naive about global dynamics. The more realistic of our citizens recognized the possibilities, particularly in the realm of international politics, but even those cautious thinkers saw the United States as an especially blessed nation with an obligation to share with those less fortunate around the world.

Now we are beginning to suspect that we may never have been as ingenious as everyone else might have thought. We have suffered our first two military setbacks in Korea and Vietnam and a number of minor ones in widely diverse locations, including Cuba and Lebanon. Our power is constantly challenged, our educational system has become more than a little suspect, our minority groups contend that they have not been allowed to make much progress, and our real income for consumer spending by the average citizen has fallen slowly but steadily for some time.

Currently, our two most embarrassing failures are our increasing inability to hold our own in the highly competitive atmosphere of free world trade and our seeming powerlessness to bring our deficit spending, both domestic and foreign, under control. Unfavorable trade and national budget imbalances have become almost routine, it seems, and more and more of our leaders are predicting a crisis or even doom if we can not stabilize our economic affairs.

There is only one positive and desirable way to do this: Our workforce must become more productive. The only alternative is a continued economic demise, which will ultimately lead to national military and cultural deterioration. Not only is our own standard of living at stake, our leadership on the world stage is endangered. Economic powerlessness equates with political powerlessness. Whether we openly admit it or not, we are a bit frightened and very disappointed in ourselves.

We are only beginning to assess—and accept—how all this happened. For a time we told ourselves that we were suffering under a temporary condition that would adjust itself soon. Now we have begun to suspect that the causes of our problems run deep within our society, express themselves with great complexity, and offer no quick or easy solutions.

Obviously, there must be a diagnosis of the cause of these difficulties before any solutions can be created and effected. At the risk of oversimplifying, perhaps our current national economic malaise can best be explained by comparison to the situation in another country, whose economy has improved at our expense. One need look no further than the dramatic reversal of economic roles of the United States and Japan in the last forty years.

In 1945 Japan was our defeated enemy and was prostrate before our occupation forces. The country's industry was destroyed, the economy crippled, and an estimated 60 percent of all buildings had been demolished or damaged beyond use. More than ninety million people were living in a geographical area approximately the size of California, and only 20 percent of that land was arable. Natural resources were minimal, and the central government was nonfunctional.

The general outlook for that nation was bleak, indeed, but in twenty years Japan had made a complete recovery in every respect, and was experiencing substantial, and even dramatic, prosperity. It had become established as a leader in industry and world trade in that short period of time, and was already recording a yearly surplus in commercial exchanges with the United States. During the following twenty years that surplus grew so significantly that many economists began to call it a transfer of wealth from this nation to that one.

Several factors may have contributed to the economic reversal of roles between the two former enemies: (1) the destruction of Japanese industry during the war necessitated the building of modern, more efficient factories; (2) Japan had no clear investment of resources in self-defense, since the new constitution outlawed war and the United States, in effect, was paying for Japan's national security; and (3) the homogeneous society, culture, and tradition made that country's educational system more effective and technological advances more rapid. There are many other theories, of course, advanced by a variety of experts.

However, there is almost universal agreement on one point: the Japanese, in the late 1940s, built their recovery on the basic foundations of education and mental discipline, for, lacking natural resources, they were forced to depend on human resources. This example strongly suggests that the United States can become more productive only if it, too, dedicates itself to the development of human potential. Our natural resources no longer give a decided advantage in production and world trade, and our labor force is obviously losing in the competition with those of many other countries.

A complete treatment of the thesis outlined above would demand a weighty and lengthy discourse, because the social, educational, governmental, and economic implications are many and diverse. However, it is the purpose of this publication to describe briefly the nature of the two-year college and its contribution to American society at this time. The authors are bold enough to suggest that the greatest burden—or privilege—of cultural and economic change in this nation for the 1990s will be placed on the twelve hundred or so community, technical, and junior colleges. They further hold that the educational and productive shortcomings of our labor force are not only inseparable but inevitably intertwined. More and more economists are saying that economic development and recovery must begin at the local two-year colleges. The authors agree with that view.

What is the nature of this completely American educational institution that has evolved in the present century? What makes it so different? How can this relatively new and unprestigious group of community-oriented institutions even dream of making such a momentous and sweeping contribution to the nation's well-being? The answers may be found in the study of the weaknesses of the labor force, a large percentage of which, educationally speaking, no longer produces and competes at the desired level internationally.

These are the educational and cultural needs that brought the two-year college into existence in the first place. Educators had known for some time that the natural break in the educational ladder is more often after the fourteenth year, not the twelfth year. Moreover, it was widely recognized, even before the technological revolution triggered by World War II and its aftermath, that many job skills not requiring a baccalaureate degree could not be delivered in the first twelve years of instruction. It became apparent that a special kind of education to fill this void, at the thirteenth and fourteenth years, would have to be delivered—locally, in immediately responsive institutions shaped by community necessities. The junior and community college movement was not a conceptual invention; it had to happen.

At this point, it must be emphasized that the evolution of these colleges mandated that they not train but educate. Nor are their "academic" courses inferior. To those who are still dubious that literature and welding can be taught together in the same institution that produces nurses and electronic technicians, please be assured that it is not only possible but absolutely necessary. There can be no logical or productive division of "liberal" and "occupational" education. This myth has handicapped the United States for too long. Nothing is more vocational than a law school, and no employer wants a technician with an uncultivated mind. The comprehensive curriculum in the two-year college was not deliberately formulated; it was shaped to meet the various needs of students and employers alike.

The two-year college is here to stay. It is what it must be—the people's college—and the numbers in the last fifty years show that clearly. Growth—from five hundred institutions in 1934 enrolling one hundred ten thousand students to some twelve hundred colleges in 1987 enrolling more than five million—is clear proof that these institutions serve exigencies that can not be met otherwise. Of course, these numbers include only credit enrollment, which is nearly matched by students taking noncredit courses. Today more than half the entering freshmen in the nation enroll in these colleges each fall.

Their institutional nature, then, is to serve their community's requirements, and they do that so well that it is safe to say that no two community colleges are exactly alike. They are the flexible, creative, and responsive arm of higher education. A program of study may flourish today with a large enrollment and be discontinued in a few years, only to be reconstituted later because community requisites demand it. And there can be no artificial efforts: if a course is not needed, students will not enroll in it. In the well-administered two-year college, business, industry, and the job market often dictate a large part of the course offerings but not the detailed content of the curriculum. That prerogative is as jealously guarded by the faculty as it is by their colleagues in the universities, but the list of courses must be responsive to the community constituency. If any part of the curriculum is not responsive, it withers.

The core of liberal arts courses not only parallels that in the universities, it is of the same quality. It must be, for many community college students will carry those credits and that body of knowledge with them when they go on to those institutions for upper-level education. But quality is not dictated by transfer. The terminal community college student must also have the very best communication, mathematical, scientific, and art education to enhance the quality of life and to ensure success at work.

The nature, mission, scope, and goals of the two-year college are difficult to separate, if, indeed, they can be separated, for the basic institutional thrust is to serve the nontraditional student. Nontraditional students are part-time and full-time, occupational and academic, old and young, preparing for a first career and preparing for a fifth, athletically oriented and disinterested in team competition, full-time employed and nonworking, motivated and mildly experimenting, residential and commuting, prosperous and existing on student aid, activities-oriented and noncommitted—and the list goes on and on because the community college is always a cross section of the community it serves. The college owes its existence to that community, by which it is dominated and shaped. Yet it maintains its academic excellence, because if the community college does not produce quality education that is salable in the labor market, it goes out of existence.

Critics are wont to say that these institutions try to be all things to all people. Not so. Community desires and needs dictate all programs. One college will act as the cultural center of its community, whereas a neighboring institution might not play that role at all. The constituency of many colleges are avid supporters of intercollegiate athletics, whereas some colleges have no athletics and want none. Some colleges have elaborate student activity programs, whereas on other campuses such programs are nonexistent. The nature of the community becomes the nature of the college, and the goals of the community become those of the college.

The purpose of this publication is to acquaint the casual reader with the services and programs of these colleges. If one accepts that the educational and production levels of our nation's labor force must be raised, if we are to compete on a par with other nations in world economic competition, it follows that this can only be done through our system of community colleges.

We need have no fear about the cultural and intellectual advancement of those who study there—it will follow naturally.

Gerald H. Fisher is president of Garland County Community College in Hot Springs, Arkansas.

ECONOMIC DEVELOPMENT

By Donald J. Donato

Economic development is defined as the maintenance or expansion of current industry and the attraction of new industry. Economic development has been greatly emphasized by all levels of government during the 1980s in reaction to the loss of industry to global competition, regional competition for the remaining industries, and the loss of heavy-manufacturing industries throughout the United States.

States and local communities have implemented a three-pronged approach to economic development. First, governments eagerly compete for new, large industries that would provide many jobs and substantial money to the local economy. The recent competition among several states for the General Motor's Saturn company is an illustration of this economic activity. Second, states have initiated mature industry policies to assist existing industries to become more competitive and thus remain in their current location. Third, government at all levels has encouraged the creation of small business. The growth in small businesses is said to account for most of the economic growth in this decade as the manufacturing sector has declined. States and local communities look to newly created small businesses to buffer the impact of the economic cycles of our manufacturing-dominated economy and to be less dependent on the manufacturing sector.

Governments market their communities and provide trained manpower to stimulate economic development. Small and rural community colleges have traditionally provided the trained manpower that local business and industry required. Early community college proponents enunciated the important relationship between the college's provision of programs and services to meet the needs of the sponsoring community and the community's allocation of resources to the college. The college was seen as the educational, social, and cultural center of their community.

ROLE OF COLLEGES IN ECONOMIC DEVELOPMENT

What types of assistance do small and rural community colleges provide to enhance the economic development efforts of their sponsoring communities? Nearly six hundred small and rural community colleges were asked to describe the role they play in the economic development effort of their communities. More than one-third of the colleges responded to the national survey, the results of which follow.

Most of the colleges indicated that their communities have embarked on economic development activities. When asked, "Does your college's service area have a local economic development agency?" 89 percent responded yes. Major economic development activities by local economic development agencies include recruiting manufacturing firms (80 percent), recruiting service industries (73 percent), recruiting small business (69 percent), assisting in business expansion (67 percent), and providing assistance to new businesses (52 percent). Clearly the sponsoring communities of the colleges are engaged in a variety of economic development activities.

About half of the colleges allied themselves with the economic development efforts of their communities. In terms of purpose, 46 percent of the colleges indicated that economic development was part of their colleges' mission statement, and 54 percent said that their colleges had goal statements involving economic development.

Yet nearly 90 percent of the colleges responded that they offered job-specific training to new or expanding industries. Since the availability of trained manpower is an essential tool in economic development, the colleges were a significant partner in this aspect of economic development. Forty-six percent reported that they provided free job-specific training, whereas 50 percent indicated that the cost was subsidized by state funds and 24 percent indicated that the cost was subsidized by their college's operating budget. This extensive training effort was evidence that the communities used the colleges' training programs to attract and maintain industry.

This training achieves two of the three major purposes of economic development cited above: attracting new industry through low-cost, job-specific training and the maintenance of current industry when this same training makes existing industry more competitive and less likely to leave an area.

The chief executive officers of the small and rural colleges were active partners with their local agencies in marketing their communities. In fact, most of them (87 percent) indicated that their activities included economic development. The chief executive officers reported that they were members of a chamber of commerce (83 percent), a team recruiting new industry (57 percent), a local or state industrial recruitment economic development board (52 percent), and a local association of industrial leaders (41 percent).

Faculty, however, were less involved in assisting their communities with economic development. Only 34 percent of the colleges indicated that service to industry is included in the job descriptions of their faculty; 45 percent felt that faculty were highly aware of their role in economic development; and 62 percent felt that their faculty attitude toward economic development was passive or underdeveloped. One reason for less faculty support for economic development may be that faculty see their role principally in the traditional role of preparation of students for the associate degree rather than the job-specific training needed by current or new industry.

The third emphasis of economic development is the encouragement of small businesses to diversify the local economy and decrease the community's dependence on the manufacturing sector. The colleges expressed significant interest in responding to the needs of small business.

A small business assistance center is operated by 40 percent of the colleges. Services offered include financial planning guidance (99 percent), demographic data collection (82 percent), feasibility studies (66 percent), venture capital information (23 percent), and incubators on or off the campus (9 percent).

Many of the services provided by the center are of the counseling variety (i.e., guidance, information, and data). Feasibility studies and the operation of an incubator, on the other hand, signify a more direct role of the college in technically assisting small businesses. It is in their small business technical assistance that some small and rural colleges have departed from the community college's traditional role of solely providing skilled manpower. Colleges providing technical assistance see themselves as direct agents of economic development in their communities.

Before undertaking such a role, the college needs to assure itself and the community that it is providing a service that is complementary rather than competing with other economic development agencies in the community. Duplication of services would be a wasteful use of scarce resources. The data in this survey suggested that 60 percent of the colleges did not see a role for themselves in providing such direct economic development activities. Each college needs to determine the role it should play in the economic development of its community. A review of each college's choices may assist in this determination.

AN ECONOMIC DEVELOPMENT MODEL FOR SMALL AND RURAL COLLEGES

Economic development requires the marketing of a community and the provision of skilled manpower. Today many community colleges are assisting economic development by providing graduates of their degree and certificate programs to local industry. As part of this effort, the colleges offer courses in conjunction with other training programs, such as apprenticeship training or employer tuition incentive programs.

The colleges can also offer job-specific, customized employee training to current industry and should indicate a willingness to do the same for new industry. Under these circumstances, the college would be assisting current industry in being more competitive and assisting the community in marketing its area to prospective industry.

The colleges can further enhance economic development by supporting small business. The college has several choices as to the extent of its assistance. The community college can provide counseling to new entrepreneurs, by offering guidance, general information, and statistical data. At this level the college provides access to sources of information that the entrepreneurs can use to create small businesses on their own. The college can also provide direct technical assistance to the entrepreneur. Services at this level include marketing analysis, creation of a business plan, or financial packaging, resulting in, for example, a study on the marketability of a product, an application suitable for a commercial bank loan, or an application for one or more of the state and/or federal capitalization programs. Frequently these same services can be used by existing small businesses that want to expand or are in danger of failing.

At the highest level of involvement the college can operate its own incubator facility or be a part of one. An incubator provides centralized supportive services to small business such as accounting, secretarial, communication, maintenance, and security, as well as technical assistance services.

This level of direct support of economic development requires extensive analysis and commitment by the college and the sponsoring community. For example, the college may provide counseling or technical assistance services within a community-based incubator program and avoid the extensive commitment that a college-operated incubator would entail. This arrangement preserves the team approach to economic development and ensures that the college is perceived as supporting the community's efforts. Some colleges have created incubators on campus, remodeling currently unused facilities or building new ones. Others have formed incubators off campus, leasing available space within the community. Frequently these incubators limit the kind of business that can be operated; determine the life of the business (typically three years); restrict the type of product the incubated business can provide; and require a commitment of the small business to settle eventually in the sponsoring community when it leaves the incubator facility. Some colleges insist that the employees of the small business involved in the incubator enroll in entrepreneurial education courses.

Each small and rural college must examine the needs and resources available in the community to determine its role in economic development. The model and survey data presented within this chapter provide a schema within which small and rural colleges can define their proper roles in the community's economic development efforts.

Donald J. Donato is president of Niagara County Community College in Sanborn, New York.

CULTURAL AND CIVIC RESPONSIBILITY

By Marvin W. Weiss

Much has been written and said about the cultural and civic responsibility of community, technical, and junior colleges. Until 1987 the American Association of Community and Junior Colleges had little information regarding what, specifically, the small and rural community colleges are doing in the area of cultural and civic responsibility.

During 1986/87, under the auspices of AACJC, the Commission on Small/Rural Community Colleges surveyed nearly six hundred small and rural colleges to determine what kind of cultural and civic involvements are prevalent. Almost half of the colleges responded. This survey included the following questions:

1. What is the priority at your college for cultural programs or activities that you offer?
2. Is your college viewed as a cultural center in your service area? If yes, list some activity examples of the past *two* years which will show that your institution influences culture in your service area.
3. What is your priority at your college for civic programs or activities that you offer?
4. Is your college viewed as a civic center in your service area? If yes, list activity examples from the past *two* years that will show you are a civic influence in your service area.

In response to question one, 125 colleges (56 percent) believed that the cultural programs or activities at their institutions were a high priority. Seventy colleges (31 percent) believed that cultural programs or activities had a low priority, and twenty-eight (12.6 percent) believed that there was no priority for cultural programs or activities at their institutions.

Community colleges certainly are a significant factor in being providers for cultural involvement in their communities. Those colleges that put a high priority on cultural and civic responsibilities were consistently and constantly involved in their communities, often through art councils and other civic groups. These colleges put resources into their budgets to finance and sponsor many of the cultural programs and activities. Nevertheless, that only half of the responding colleges believed that the cultural programs and activities had a high priority would seem to indicate a need for improvement by these institutions in making a cultural impact within their own service districts.

Question two on the survey asked if the college was viewed as a cultural center. One hundred fifty-eight colleges (67 percent) viewed their institutions as cultural centers, seventy-five colleges (32 percent) did not, and two respondents did not answer that question at all.

Question three asked about the college's priority regarding civic programs or activities. One hundred twenty-nine colleges (56 percent) viewed their institutions as having a high priority in offering civic programs or activities. Sixty-one colleges (27 percent) indicated that civic programs or activities were a low priority, and thirty-nine (13 percent) indicated that there was no priority listed for their institutions.

In response to question four, which asked if the college was viewed as a civic center, 114 colleges (50 percent) viewed their institution as civic centers. One hundred nine colleges (47 percent) indicated that they were not viewed as civic centers, and nine (3 percent) did not answer the question at all. Since more than half the colleges felt that the priority was high and only half of them were viewed as civic centers by the public, the colleges need to improve their civic influence.

It is difficult to make generalizations about all small and rural community colleges and about how they view their institutions as cultural and/or civic centers. In these difficult times economics in rural areas has a tremendous influence on what two-year colleges can and will do in their communities regarding cultural and civic programs. Nevertheless, there are some excellent ways that, without much financial investment, small and rural colleges can become more viable community resources.

Following is a sampling of cultural activities sponsored by some colleges:

- Art exhibits featuring paintings and photographs of high school and college students, professional staff, and community artists, and professional exhibits brought in from other cities or states;
- Theater productions presented by college students, and community and professional theater productions brought to the community by the college;
- Series of lectures, on various cultural aspects, brought to the community;
- Dance and art classes involving college students and community members;
- Tours of historical and cultural sites;
- Symphony and chamber orchestra productions, solo recitals, and performances by local bands and choral groups in addition to concerts presented by the college's own band and choral groups;
- Bilingual educational programs featuring live entertainment;
- Fashion shows;
- Museum displays of artifacts;
- Field trips to metropolitan areas;
- Cultural TV programs presented through the college's community service or community education divisions;
- International dinners for students and/or visitors;

- Travel tours and travel courses;
- Celebrations of such holidays as Martin Luther King Day;
- Summer programs in outdoor theater and in dance;
- Film festivals as well as fine arts festivals;
- Book-of-the-month clubs with regularly featured book reviewers;
- Band and choir competition for high school students.

According to the survey, there was a distinct lack of involvement by the colleges with the local arts council or arts agency in their districts. Either the respondents did not feel this was important or they do not work that closely with arts agencies. Nevertheless, all rural and small community and junior colleges should be looking for ways to work with local arts agencies to enhance their cultural center approach in their communities.

In question 4, the college was asked if it was viewed as a civic center. That only half the colleges responded in the affirmative would seem to indicate that many more small and rural colleges should work toward a better civic center image.

Following is a sampling of civic events that some colleges have sponsored:

- Athletic events;
- Seminars dealing with civic problems;
- Public speakers relating to the civic area;
- High school graduations and proms on campus;
- Conferences on women in the workplace and Latin American issues, and forums on immigrants and refugees;
- Designation of college as a Red Cross emergency center;
- State, county, and city government meetings;
- Workshops for city and county employees;
- Election coverage through the college's own television network;
- Fund-raising and charity drives;
- Food drives and blood drives;
- As participants in AACJC's Building Better Boards project, involvement with area nonprofit boards;
- Boys' Club and United Way campaigns;
- Sites for voter registration;
- Area sites for economic development training.

It is obvious that the community colleges have a tremendous challenge before them. Much can be done and should be done to enhance the cultural and civic image of small and rural community colleges in particular. When only half the colleges view themselves as cultural and/or civic centers, then the time for change has come. Community colleges throughout this country must realize and uphold their cultural and civic responsibilities.

Marvin W. Weiss is president of Northeastern Junior College in Sterling, Colorado.

HIGH SCHOOL CONNECTIONS AND PARTNERSHIPS

By Billy Thames

The importance of the role to be played by the community and junior colleges of America by forming partnerships with area high schools, business, industry, and labor is probably the most overlooked and neglected responsibility of these institutions today. During the last few years it has become increasingly important for all segments of government and various agencies that make up government to work closer together to bring about the change that is so vital and necessary for economic vitality. Just a few years back, agencies and institutions could and did survive without this close connection.

The last few years have not been good ones for the American economy. The federal deficit has risen to heights that were unheard of in the past. In fact, it was unthinkable that this could happen to a strong and productive nation like the United States. The United States has entered into a global economy where cheap labor, government subsidies, and cost-effective automated production systems have permitted countries such as Korea, Japan, and China to dominate markets that were exclusively American just a few years ago. These countries and others have cut drastically into the American share of the market, and the prospects that they will continue to command healthy shares of this market appear to be quite strong.

Just twenty years ago one could expect to wait fifteen years to translate invention into application in the workplace; now it takes an average of three years. When looking at the changes that have taken place in the automobile industry with the addition of computer-controlled robots, estimated to be growing at the rate of fifty thousand per year, it can be immediately recognized that the U.S. economy is gearing up to compete in the marketplace. The nation must do a better job of using, coordinating, and supporting the systems that can improve its competitive edge.

America has always looked to its educational system when changes were needed. During the last few years this system, which has trained so many Americans for jobs, has not kept pace with the changes that have been taking place. The rapid change that is occurring in the marketplace was not projected; therefore, education at all levels has lost some of its luster. It is time for all levels of the U.S. educational system to move out front and provide the trained manpower that is so desperately needed to fill the jobs that are available today. It is estimated that $30 billion is spent

17

each year by the U.S. public and private employers to educate and train their employees. In addition to this cost, it is estimated that the Department of Defense spends some $50 billion on education and training each year. These facts, and a growing list of statistics, tell us that business as usual will not get the job done any longer. If the educational system of this country is going to maintain its respect, it must take the lead in training Americans to fill the jobs that are available today.

HIGH SCHOOL STUDENT IN NEED

In his book, *The Neglected Majority*, Dr. Dale Parnell points out that about 27 percent of high school students drop out before graduation and that this percentage has increased by 5 percent during the last ten years. He further indicates that only about one-half of those who graduate move immediately into some type of postsecondary training. Of this group, only 26 percent complete a baccalaureate degree. The patterns being forecast by these students should cause educators to be concerned.

A national longitudinal study of the class of 1980 indicated the following percentages of enrollment in the various programs of study: academic (college prep), 37 percent; vocational, 19 percent; general, 42 percent; and unreported, 2 percent. Further examination of this study indicates that approximately two-thirds of the high school dropouts came from the general education program. Community and junior college administrators should be working with area high school districts to provide the two-plus-two associate degree or similar programs to help remedy this situation. This approach is being advocated by the Southern Regional Education Board, Dr. Dale Parnell, and many other leading educators today.

OPPORTUNITIES FOR COMMUNITY AND JUNIOR COLLEGES

Articulation agreements between the college and area high schools head the list of partnership efforts between these institutions. Many of these agreements are in courses offered through the vocational-technical programs of the area high schools and community and junior colleges. Articulation between the various educational levels has many benefits for which students are the most important beneficiaries. Through these articulation agreements students who take high school programs are not penalized by having to retake courses and are encouraged to prepare themselves for higher-order jobs. The institution can also benefit from articulation. It can minimize the use of personnel, facilities, and equipment. Resources can be directed to other pressing needs. The society also benefits because the graduates are more productive, less dependent, and because the dropout rate is reduced.

Currently, there are a number of community and junior colleges that have established, or are considering the establishment of, articulation programs. The need for such effort is emphasized by the large number of high school students who drop out and do not achieve the skills they need to survive in today's job market. Through articulation agreements the student is given credit toward a certificate or an associate degree for coursework completed in high school.

In addition to articulation agreements, many colleges provide other early enrollment programs. These programs have many titles, but all serve the same purpose: to provide students with the opportunities and education for early entrance into the labor force. These programs include two-plus-two agreements, concurrent enrollment agreements, cooperative early education agreements, and coordinated credit agreements.

Cooperative arrangements for use of facilities, staff, and equipment provide colleges and area high schools with additional opportunities for cooperation. The colleges teach academic courses and provide laboratory facilities and expensive computer equipment for area high schools that could not otherwise afford the services. In return the area schools provide the college with classroom space for adult basic education programs and night and off-campus classes. Faculty members serve both institutions as full-time employees for one and part-time employees for the other or may serve part-time for both institutions.

Schools at all levels have formed consortia that allow them to work together in a cooperative manner. The results have indicated that all parties are happy and the parties are recipients of training that is beneficial to them. Partnerships of this nature enhance the positions of the educational institutions and provide a very important image that all school systems work so hard to obtain.

RESULTS OF A SURVEY

In a recent survey conducted by the Commission on Small/Rural Community Colleges through the American Association of Community and Junior Colleges (AACJC), it was found that approximately 60 percent of the colleges responding had some type of cooperative arrangement with the area high schools of their service district. Over forty-six separate programs were listed. The programs ranged from a two-plus-two program to programs that taught chemistry and physics at the high school level and, in one case, a program that taught area high school English faculty in specialized areas.

The University of Mississippi, working with the Mississippi junior college system, has trained the junior college instructors to instruct area junior high and high school teachers in the art of "writing across the curriculum." Starting in the fall of 1987, the junior college instructor will be teaching district English teachers, free of charge, to improve the writing programs in their schools.

This is just one example of what can occur when all levels of education work together. This work is being provided by the Matsushita Foundation, thereby providing an added link to the partnership.

In reviewing the Small/Rural Commission survey, it was interesting to study the following reasons that were given for establishing partnerships.

The study showed that the greatest influence for the community and junior college becoming involved in a partnership was that it was part of the institutional mission (35 percent). Request from the state ranked second (25 percent), while changing society (20 percent), unemployment (14 percent), and part of a consortium (4 percent) also influenced participation in partnerships.

Partnerships between area high schools also provide training programs for local business and industry, and are discussed later in this chapter. Government agencies are included in partnership agreements with local community and junior colleges. Colleges provide training programs for local hospitals, state highway departments, prisons, and the postal service.

The recent survey also asked for advantages and disadvantages that must be addressed as an institution considers partnerships with area high schools. Among the advantages listed were the following:

1. Saving in resources;
2. Better service to the students;
3. Better communication among agencies;
4. Improvement of college image and visibility;
5. Provision for needed services;
6. High visibility;
7. High job placement;
8. Faculty awareness of new technology;
9. Provision for contacts in placement of graduates;
10. Exposure of more people to the college programs;
11. Increased enrollment;
12. College development of new programs and markets;
13. Enrichment of high school curriculum; and
14. Securing new industry.

Among the disadvantages were the following:

1. Lack of resources;
2. Lack of time and facilities;
3. Lack of cooperation between institutions;
4. Overload of faculty and staff;
5. Difficulty in accessing needs;
6. Faculty resistance;
7. Administrative, government, and political red tape;
8. Lack of flexibility;
9. Lack of communication;
10. Disciplinary problems;
11. Lack of coordination;
12. Faculty jealousy and protection of turf;
13. Duplication of services; and
14. High cost of training.

It is interesting to note that these advantages and disadvantages paralleled the findings of a study conducted by Dr. Philip R. Day, Jr., in his monograph titled *In Search of Community College Partnerships*, which was published in 1985.

The final question in the survey asked for recommendations that community and junior college personnel should consider in developing partnerships with district high schools. Over seventy-seven replies were included on the survey. Listed below is a condensed list of these recommendations:

1. Do a good job of planning, then jump in; start early;
2. Utilize advisory committees; let each partner participate;
3. Develop an open, honest relationship;
4. Recognize limitation of time, space, and resources;
5. Spell out responsibilities of each party; have a good contract;
6. Start program with best personnel and expand from there;
7. Be flexible; cultivate a thick skin and be patient;
8. Provide adequate staff and facilities;
9. Deliver what is promised;
10. Have support of the politicians, faculty, and staff;
11. Don't be afraid to take a risk;
12. Do a good needs analysis;
13. Don't duplicate services;
14. Establish accountability methods before starting;
15. Be practical;
16. Admit when expectations are beyond your reach;
17. Admit to disappointments but emphasize successes; and
18. Get in; the benefits will become apparent.

Most colleges fail in this area because they try to rely on their regular credit-course faculty and administrators or, worse, on their continuing-education dean. Successful business-industry-labor partnerships require an entirely new and different administrative unit, staffed by quick-response people and led by an aggressive, industry-oriented person who reports directly to the president. This has been pretty much the formula of success in Illinois.

The field of partnership and connections with the district high schools offers one of the most exciting challenges that has been presented to the community and junior colleges since their beginning.

PARTNERSHIPS WITH SMALL BUSINESS AND INDUSTRY

According to information published by AACJC on partnerships with small businesses, 80 percent of small businesses fail within the first five years of operation; even more significant, 50 percent of those businesses fail within the first year. Therefore, it is imperative that small businesses receive early assistance to maximize their chances for success and survival.

Early assistance is currently being provided through partnership arrangements between small businesses and community and junior colleges on a limited basis.

The beginnings of national, state, and local partnership initiatives have been seen already. The Sears-Roebuck Foundation has provided funds for the AACJC to sponsor the Keeping America Working program, which provides training and retraining resources for partnerships with small business and industry.

Some states are now beginning to address the need to coordinate a central plan for economic growth and development. The Senate Finance Committee of the Mississippi Legislature saw the need in August 1986 for some group to take a leadership role in the formulation of an economic development plan for the state. That committee called for various agencies across the state to submit proposals for what role each of them could play in an overall plan of economic development. As a result, the Mississippi Junior College Association prepared a proposal that led to the establishment of the Mississippi Junior College Economic Development Foundation. The advisory board for this foundation is composed of selected business leaders from each of the fifteen junior college districts throughout the state. There are fourteen major goals and activities for the foundation, such as industrial training, entrepreneurship courses and workshops, short-term skills training, adult literacy programs, technical assistance to secondary vocational centers and programs, and local establishment and management of business incubators.

Business incubator programs are an example of partnerships that are currently working on the local level. During the critical early growth period of small businesses, overhead often determines the success or failure of those businesses. These partnerships provide an incubator-like environment (office and manufacturing space) that allows new businesses to be initiated and then nurtured through below-market overhead costs until the businesses are strong enough to move into their own facilities.

Other examples of partnerships with small business include job training start-up programs, small business resource centers, and in-service support and training services. All of these areas tend to be more successful when a full-time industrial coordinator is assigned by the community college to work directly with industry as a liaison.

The two-year college is in a unique position to provide the linkage of educational services so desperately needed by business and industry for flexible, custom-designed training and retraining programs. This enables business and industry to reap the benefits of cost-effective professional-level training for their employees. Appreciating the potential of this service, the business and industry community has extended the hand of partnership to the two-year college. It is incumbent upon the community and junior college to expand and enhance the concept of cooperation between business and industry and the education community. In order to fulfill that role, the two-year college must address the major misconceptions that tend to impede such relationships. A lack of communication is the major cause for misconceptions; therefore, effective communication must be the key to any effort to overcome this problem. According to Philip R. Day (1985), these misconceptions include image, credibility, high cost of training, and lack of college commitment.

Since its inception, the two-year college has been plagued with the distorted image of the "extended high school" or a "second-rate college." This image is partly the result of perceptions formulated in the early history of the two-year college. Also, some in the business community have a lack of respect for the practicality of courses offered, which has contributed to the poor image of the two-year college.

The credibility of the two-year college relates very closely to its image, which is directly related to the understanding of the community about the college and its mission. Community and junior colleges have matured over the years and have evolved into a comprehensive community service institution. As a result, their mission now includes services to all segments of the community; this mission is matched by a total commitment to providing educational services appropriate to the needs of the constituencies.

The cost of training personnel at the community and junior college is very reasonable, sometimes nominal, in comparison to private-sector training. Although the cost to provide training, even at the two-year college, is sometimes high for single companies with small numbers of employees, training in the private business sector or at a university would be much greater.

When two-year colleges place a high priority on communicating their comprehensiveness to the community, misconceptions pertaining to cost and commitment will be dispelled. As a consequence, the image and credibility of these institutions will also be heightened.

The contemporary two-year institution is becoming a major national training resource, and according to the Keeping America Working literature, it is doing for an information age what the land-grant university has done for an agricultural and industrial era. With the necessary resources, talent, and experience, the two-year college can meet the future needs of an expanding information age by concentrating on major criteria, which may be briefly summarized through the following terms: prepare, provide, respond, offer, help, promote, and participate.

The community college is now in a position to address national, state, and local economic problems; by doing so it will make a major contribution to the improvement of the quality of life and enhance and strengthen the human resources of the nation. The resources are available, the mechanism is in place, the time is right, the challenge is ours.

REFERENCES

Baliles, Gerald L. "Meeting the Economic Challenges of Today." *Trustee Quarterly* (Winter 1986–87).

Brock, William E. "Futureshock: The American Work Force in the Year 2000." *Community, Technical, and Junior College Journal* (February/March 1987).

Day, Philip. *In Search of Community College Partnerships.* Keeping America Working Series No. 2. (Washington, D.C.: Community College Press, 1985).

Deegan, William L., and Dale Tillery. "Toward A 5th Generation of Community Colleges." *Community, Technical, and Junior College Journal* (April/May 1987).

Economic Development and the Community College. Research and Development Series No. 251 (Columbus, Ohio: National Center for Research in Vocational Education, 1984).

Halfway Home and a Long Way to Go. The Report of the 1986 Commission on the Future of the South. Southern Growth Policies Board.

Hill, John P. "Funds for Excellence: A College Faculty/Industry Partnership." *Community College Review* (May 1985).

Illinois Trustee 17, No. 2 (September 1986).

Keeping America Working Through Technical Education Partnerships with High Schools and Colleges. American Association of Community and Junior Colleges and Association of Community College Trustees.

Keeping America Working Through Partnerships with Major Business/Industry Employers and Labor Unions. American Association of Community and Junior Colleges and Association of Community College Trustees.

Keeping America Working Through Partnerships with Small Business. American Association of Community and Junior Colleges and Association of Community College Trustees.

Parnell, Dale. *The Neglected Majority.* (Washington, D.C.: Community College Press, 1985).

Responding to the Challenge of a Changing American Economy. Progress Report on the Sears Partnership Development Fund. (Washington, D.C.: American Association of Community and Junior Colleges and Association of Community College Trustees, 1985).

Resource and Coordinating Units for Economic Development. A Concept Paper of the Mississippi Junior College Association. August 29, 1986.

Scott, Robert. "Proven Partners: Business, Government, and Education." *Community, Technical, and Junior College Journal* (December/January 1986–87).

Warmbrod, Catherine, and James Long. "College Bound or Bust: Ten Principles for Articulation." *Community, Technical, and Junior College Journal* (October/November 1986).

SUMMARY

The opportunities for the community and the junior colleges of America are at an all-time high today. Never has the nation's business, industry, and labor faced the challenges of change like today. The global markets, foreign competition, and the quick application of invention to the marketplace have forced changes on the economy that were unexpected. Business-as-usual will not get the job done today.

The community and junior colleges can come to the aid of business, industry, and labor by forming partnerships with high schools, business, industry, and labor. Because of the flexibility and the highly skilled teaching force in place, these institutions can seize this golden opportunity that knocks at their doors today. Partnerships at all levels have been advocated by the president of the United States, industrialists, and leading educators.

Serious attention must be given to many problems that exist, including communication, planning, coordination, and financial revenues, in addition to commitment for all parties.

Educators throughout the nation advocate partnerships to curtail high school dropouts as well as to provide a highly competitive work force.

The community and junior colleges of America can move out front if they seize the opportunities available to them today.

Billy B. Thames is president of Copiah-Lincoln Junior College in Wesson, Mississippi.

Literacy Practices

By Jerry W. Young

That illiteracy is a substantial problem in America would seem to need no additional documentation. Debates go on as to whom to blame—parents, public schools, the high immigration rates, etc.—and people quibble over just how many are illiterate. There are obvious problems of definition, and there are those who enjoy the debate over definition more than the action of directly helping others to read, write, and compute.

The rhetoric surrounding illiteracy and remediation would lead the average person to believe that this is a problem of recent origin. The fact is that college faculty have complained each and every year about the poor academic preparation of their students since Harvard was founded in the 1600s. "The Yale Report in 1828 called for an end to the admission of students with 'defective preparation'" (Brier 1984).

Archie E. Lapointe, executive director of the National Assessment of Educational Progress (an office of Educational Testing Service), put the literacy issue in perspective in commenting upon a study (1986) done by his office:

> This study inventories the literacy skills of America's young adults, ages 21–25. By yesterday's standards, the news is good: 95% can read and understand the printed word. In terms of tomorrow's needs, there is cause for concern: Only a very small percentage can understand complex material.

In other words, the problem is not literacy itself, but change—a changing, more competitive world where knowledge-based skills are the resources that drive advanced economies. The acceptable standard for being functionally literate is rising.

Literacy has become an issue of major proportions for employers. The Business Council for Effective Literacy has published a brochure titled "Functional Illiteracy Hurts Business." On the front of the brochure in bold type is:

> 27 million adult Americans can't read or write well enough to—
> - fill out a job application
> - understand the label on a medicine bottle
> - make full use of their native ability to lead productive and satisfying lives
> - exercise the responsibilities of citizenship.

It is a powerful statement, and yet anyone who has witnessed firsthand the daily painful struggle of the illiterate knows much more poignantly the tragedy of the illiterate in a complex society.

In May of 1983 Education Services of the American Council of Life Insurance sponsored a national workshop on Functional Literacy and the Workplace. The titles of the presentations of the conference proceedings illuminate the concern of employers over literacy: "Illiteracy: The Cost to the Nation," "Basic Skills in the U.S. Workforce," "Basic Skills in Financial Services." The American Management Association published a booklet, *Workplace Literacy*, in 1986 with these chapter titles: "If Everyone Can Read, Why Are There So Many Illiterates?" "Workplace Schoolrooms," and "Designing Instruction for the Workplace."

In October of 1986 the Los Angeles Chamber of Commerce sponsored a one-day workshop, "Literacy: A Good Investment," which featured the publisher Harold McGraw. Mr. McGraw had taken some time off from his business to visit some of America's corporations to see firsthand how the problem of illiteracy was being confronted. He said, "Many corporations have turned their cafeterias into tutorial centers between 4:00 p.m. and 9:00 p.m. for teaching reading to their employees. When you see the sea of people in these large cafeterias busy at learning to read—it touches your heart." He went on to say, "The U.S. must have a workforce that is literate and competent and can master the new equipment of the information age if we are to compete in the world. Our standard of living for the next generation is at stake." Mr. McGraw indicated that on the average, 25 percent of the employees in America's corporations had literacy problems of the magnitude that they could not take advantage of company training programs.

One can not escape the conclusion that the literacy issue is closely linked with the broader issue of economic development: of the survival of an economic way of life. Community colleges have not only contributed substantially to delivery of literacy services, especially since the early 1960s, but have more recently become very involved in seeking solutions to economic development problems.

The National Center for Developmental Education at Appalachian State University in Boone, North Carolina, has identified over one hundred sixty-five exemplary developmental education programs nationally. The center receives more than two thousand requests annually for assistance. Of the exemplary programs cited, seventy-nine were in two-year colleges. The selection of exemplary programs was dependent upon institutions nominating themselves. An inspection of the list of two-year institutions will reveal that many well-known institutions with strong developmental programs did not nominate themselves. In spite of this weakness, the list does show two things: that two-year colleges are doing their part in the challenge of literacy, and that the literacy problem is not unique to community, technical, and junior colleges.

The authors of the *National Directory of Exemplary Programs in Developmental Education* (1986) concluded from their review of programs, "If developmental education originated as a knee-jerk response to a desperate need, it has come full circle to represent one of the most systematically planned and best monitored enterprises in postsecondary education."

STUDIES OF TWO-YEAR COLLEGES

In the spring of 1986, AACJC conducted a national survey of its membership on the topic of adult literacy programs. Of the 1,222 institutions surveyed, 259 returned the questionnaires for a 21.2 percent return. The results of that survey are interesting, in particular:

1. Noncredit programs compose the majority of college literacy programs (141) as opposed to credit programs (91).
2. A median enrollment in formal programs was 250 per year.
3. Courses offered through newspapers enrolled 600 annually.
4. Cooperative efforts existed with high schools, literacy groups, state government, businesses, and churches.
5. While more than 15 percent (median) of the community population were in need of literacy training, only 5 percent (median) of that portion of the population took advantage of literacy offerings.
6. The typical student in these programs was female, between twenty-one and thirty years of age, Caucasian, with a family income of between $5,000 and $10,000 annually (in other words, financially poor).

In December of 1986 AACJC mailed a comprehensive questionnaire on behalf of AACJC's Commission on Small/Rural Community Colleges. A portion of that questionnaire probed the issue of literacy practices in the nearly six hundred small and rural two-year colleges in America. *Small* is defined as those colleges with less than a headcount enrollment of twenty-five hundred. *Rural* is self-defined by colleges who perceive their service area as rural.

When one looks at a map of the United States with the standard metropolitan statistical areas (cities with at least 50,000 inhabitants) highlighted, one is impressed with the fact that close to 90 percent of the geographical area in the United States is still rural (Treadway 1984). Even though the rural areas of the United States make up the most rapidly growing segment of the population (excluding farm residents), convenience is not a characteristic of life in rural America. If higher education is present, it is most often represented in the form of a community, technical, or junior college.

In the AACJC survey of the small and rural colleges, 228 questionnaires were returned, but fifteen of these were not usable because of inadequate data. The 213 questionnaires tabulated represent a return rate of approximately 35 percent. The college headcount enrollment of the responding institutions ranged from 16 with less than 500 to thirty-six with more than 3,500. The mode (most frequent number of colleges) was in the 1,000 to 2,000 headcount range (Treadway 1984).

The population of the service area served by these colleges ranged from thirteen with less than 25,000 to fourteen with more than 250,000. The mode was in the 100,000 to 150,000 range. Interestingly, twenty-six of the colleges did not know the population size of their service areas.

For purposes of the questionnaire, literacy was broadly defined as "programs, courses, or services that exist to improve basic skills of underprepared students." When asked to identify staffing for the literacy effort, it was obvious that twenty-one responses referred to the college as a whole and eight did not respond to this item. Of the remaining responses, the staffing pattern below emerged:

Position	None	Part-time	1	2	3	4	5	6	7	8+
Administrator	33	52	63	11						
Full-time faculty	42	5	49	29	20	19	7	8	6	7
Adjunct faculty	56		16	20	18	9	8	6	3	44
Paraprofessionals	82	3	37	19	13	9	4	3		10
Clerical	65	13	63	23	6	1	1			1
Student assistants	84		10	6	12	7	3	7	1	30
Volunteers	94		3	6	2	1	5	3		39

There is a heavy reliance on one part-time and one full-time administrator, one to four full-time faculty, one to three adjunct faculty, one or two paraprofessionals, and one to two clerical staff for staffing literacy programs. Some interesting exceptions exist. One college reported using sixty-three adjunct faculty in a rather large program. A number of colleges reported using large numbers of volunteers (thirteen colleges ranged from 50 to 273 volunteers) even though the majority of colleges reporting this data (ninety-four) still do not utilize this resource.

The enrollment in literacy classes ranged from a low of 20 to a high of 2,997 with an average of 451.7 and a median of 266. The frequency distribution of enrollment was trimodal.

Enrollment	No. of Colleges Reporting
100	10
200	11
300	11

There were forty-two blanks on this item. The really surprising data are the huge range.

The following data were tabulated on the question "What is the responsibility of the public schools in your area for adult education?":

Total responsibility   —   8
No responsibility   —   83
Shared responsibility   — 101
Blank   —   33
Other   —   4

It is noteworthy that in only eight situations do the colleges have no responsibility for adult literacy because the public school responsibility is total. In almost all instances the colleges have total responsibility or it is shared with the public schools. The "other" responses referred to situations where the responsibility was shared with other groups, such as local literacy councils.

In terms of literacy courses offered, the following data emerged:

Credit   — 123
Noncredit   — 153
ESL   — 95
ABE   — 141
GED   — 141
Developmental/remedial   — 192
Study skills   — 171
Other:
  Career exploration   — 10
  Adult high school   —   3
  Tutorial   —   2
  Blank   — 21

As in the earlier AACJC study, noncredit courses predominate. What is most impressive is the 192 responses under developmental/remedial, which is a composite category that probably includes offerings in other categories on the list. The number of colleges offering ESL, ABE, GED, developmental/remedial, and study skills is certainly testimony to the comprehensiveness of programs in small and rural colleges and also the colleges' commitment to serving adults with literacy needs.

Item 5 asked for information on the types of literacy support services provided:

Tutorial   — 188
Assessment   — 197
Advising   — 198
Course placement   — 179
Counseling   — 191
Resource
  program   — 105
Other   —   5
Blank   — 21

Again, the large percentage of colleges offering these services and the number of them being offered at any one college is very impressive.

Item 6 asked the colleges to identify the percent of instruction offered in three different modes (individualized, small group, and regular classes). Twelve colleges did not respond to this item and twenty-two simply checked the items and did not indicate percentages. This item is difficult to summarize as no clear pattern emerged; all three modes are used. The extremes are more interesting. Seven of the colleges did not use individualized instruction, thirty-one did not use small groups, and twenty-three did not use regular classes. On the other hand, ten of the colleges used only individualized instruction, two used only small groups, and six used only regular classes. The modes for individualized instruction are 10 percent (twenty-two colleges) and 50 percent (twenty colleges), for small group 20 to 30 percent (forty-five colleges), and for regular classes it is fairly evenly distributed across the percentages with a mode of 50 percent (twenty-two colleges).

The significant reliance on regular classes as a delivery system is surprising, given the research that strongly suggests small class sizes are much more effective for those needing remedial work. This may simply be an economic fact, since regular classes are the least costly way of delivering education.

Item 7 asked the colleges to identify the percent of time a particular instructional methodology was used in literacy education. As with item 6, the data collected here is more interesting at the extremes and in this case the lower extreme is more significant. Twenty of the colleges did not use the lecture method, twenty-four did not use computer-assisted instruction, fifty-three did not use mediated instruction, and twenty-nine did not use paper-and-pencil programmed material. The modes for each method are reflected below:

Method	No. of Colleges	Percentages
Lecture	74	10–40 (48 above 40%)
Computer-assisted	97	5–30 (16 above 30%)
Mediated	48	5–20 (38 above 20%)
Programmed paper and pencil	50	20–40 (34 above 40%)

The data suggest that the colleges rely on a little of each approach, with a small percentage of the colleges relying heavily on only one method. The availability of multiple approaches must be advantageous to students, if some diagnosis is done to assess the best approach for each student.

Item 8 asked the colleges to estimate the need for literacy education in their service area as a percentage of the population of their service area.

> More than 25%   — 95
> More than 20–24%   — 52
> More than 14–20%   — 30
> More than 8–13%   — 29

Less than 8% — 8
Blank — 14

These data seem close to the information about the percentage of the American population in general needing literacy education. Some respondents indicated they were guessing and had no idea what the level of need was in their area.

The colleges were also asked to identify the percentage of the need in their district being met by their colleges, the public schools, or others. One college said it was meeting none of the need, twenty-seven said they were meeting 100 percent of the need (which is very difficult to believe), and thirty-three of the colleges left this blank. In reference to the public schools, seventy-three of the colleges said the public schools were meeting none of the need. The mode for the colleges meeting the need occurred between the first and twenty-fifth percentile (ninety-four colleges) and the mode for the public schools was between the first and the tenth percentile (forty colleges). The only other group (eight) mentioned with any frequency was literacy councils, meeting between 1 and 10 percent of the local need. The data suggest (apart from the twenty-seven colleges meeting 100 percent of the need) that there is still much to be done in meeting existing needs.

The colleges were asked how many used volunteers.

<u>Utilize Volunteers</u>
Yes — 84
No — 91
Blank — 30

As mentioned above, this appears to be a resource that can be more fully utilized.

The colleges were also asked if they had exemplary practices in their literacy program.

<u>Exemplary Practices</u>
Yes — 32
No — 77
Blank — 96

Some of the specific exemplary practices mentioned were Retired Senior Volunteer Program (three), volunteer programs (seven), ABE and GED programs (six), Literacy Volunteers of America (four), retired teachers (two), tutorial programs (three), Community Alliance Projects, transportation, child care, and grants (two).

One of the more interesting items asked the colleges to describe the kind of students who participate in literacy education. The descriptions are clustered, but retain words and concepts used.

Descriptions of the kinds of students in literacy programs:

Description	Frequency
1. Returning adults –late beginners, 2nd chance students –30+ years old	51
2. Low achievers –high school graduates or GED holders with deficiencies –high risk, weak basic skills, underprepared –marginal high school students, poor high school preparation –typical high school graduate lacking basic skills –students needing help in one or two subjects –skill deficient and not enrolled in regular courses –reading disability –nontraditional, not high school achievers –lower high school quartile	50
3. High school dropouts –non-high-school graduates	38
4. High school graduates through older adults –diverse, no particular type, almost all types –broad range, young adults	35
5. Minorities	22
6. Low scores on assessment tests –below eighth grade basic skill level: 8 –below twelfth grade reading level: 3 –below fourth grade basic skill level: 1 –ACT below 16 on COMP: 1 –low assessment scores: 5	18
7. Poor –lower socioeconomic level –below poverty level, welfare	14
8. Lack of confidence –poorly motivated, insecure –first-generation college students –need help adjusting to college	14
9. Unemployed	12
10. Single parents –mature women with children	8
11. ESL students	7
12. Education Opportunity Program students –specific deficiencies	7

–handicapped, developmentally disabled
–traumatic injuries

13. Employed, seeking improvement — 5
    –meet life goals
    –get better job

14. Desire to improve study skills — 3

15. Small, rural high school graduates — 2

16. Blank — 25

It is tempting to use labels to define the typical student (such as returning adult, never finished high school, low achiever, poor, minority, lacking in confidence, unemployed, single). This is not useful in helping these students. Much more important would be to assess the need they bring and to be able to advise them as to how to meet their needs.

A last question asked how the college defined literacy.

Definitions of Literacy

Description | Frequency

1. Basic skill education designed to bring students up
   to standards of regular courses — 63
   –skill-building courses
   –reading and study skills development
   –poor reading skills, can't succeed in regular courses
   –anyone needing assistance in reading, writing, and remedial courses
   –student below tenth-grade level
   –nontransfer credit
   –education provided through high school completion

2. Students who are placed by assessment — 56
   –education for persons below third-grade level: 1
   –education for persons below fourth-grade level: 1
   –education for persons below sixth-grade level: 10
   –education for persons below seventh-grade level: 1
   –education for persons below eighth-grade level: 8
   –education for persons below ninth-grade level: 1
   –education for persons below tenth-grade level: 3
   –education for persons with less than twelfth-grade education: 7
   –math and English placement based on number of high school courses completed
   –below collegiate level
   –less than 100 course level
   –courses for those needing remedial assistance
   –entry level testing placement

3. Developmental studies/courses — 24

4. Adult Basic Education program — 21
   –survival skills
   –prepare adults to live and function in society

5. Blank — 22

6. No good definition — 15
   –no definition
   –not well defined

7. Other — 9
   –peer tutoring: 1
   –undergrads not ready for college: 3
   –intermediate course: 1
   –separate department: 1
   –minor part of basic curriculum: 1
   –not acknowledged: 1
   –students referred by faculty: 1

It can be seen from the definitions that there was a tendency to define literacy by the type of student or an assessment level, neither of which may be a useful or valid definition. Some definitions were also quite comprehensive, including, for example, more than simply instruction in reading.

Recent studies have shown that 21 percent of all four-year college freshmen need remedial work in reading; 32 percent of all two-year college freshmen need assistance. Remedial writing is needed by 24 percent of all four-year freshmen and by 33 percent of their peers in two-year colleges. Mathematics shows the greatest need for remediation: 26 percent for four-year freshmen and 39 percent for their two-year counterparts (Platt 1986). K. Patricia Cross established a long time ago that community colleges were attracting a high percentage of nontraditional students. In an in-depth study of literacy development in an unnamed community college, Richardson, Fisk, and Okun (1983) distinguished between critical literacy (requiring higher level skills of analysis, synthesis, and independent expression) and functional literacy (focusing on specific bits of factual information). The research noted that faculty and students were under severe time constraints, which contributed to a focus on functional literacy.

This author, in two informal studies in two different community colleges that had recognized individualized instruction programs in developmental education, found that the average time spent with each student in the laboratory setting each week was very low (eight minutes in one and twelve minutes in the other). The small amount of instructional time available to students either in highly enrolled individualized formats or in large classroom settings contributes to the focus on functional, as opposed to critical, literacy.

John Roueche and his colleagues have studied developmental education (literacy) in community colleges for years. One of Roueche's principles of learning is time-on-task. It would be interesting to know how many colleges know the time-on-task pattern for each student in their developmental programs.

On September 7, 1983, President Reagan established the Adult Literacy Initiative (ALI). This initiative has stimulated a number of studies and programs focusing on literacy. Yet no federal policy exists on this critical issue, where:

- one out of nine Americans can't read at all.
- 30 percent of naval recruits are functionally illiterate.
- one out of ten drivers had to have the driver's exam read to them.
- 85 percent of all juvenile offenders are illiterate.
- 65 percent of all prisoners are illiterate.
- one-third of all welfare mothers can't read.
- one-fourth of all army recruits are placed in remedial classes so they can understand manuals written at the seventh-grade level.
- 75 percent of the unemployed do not have the basic skills necessary for entry-level jobs in high-tech firms.
- 40 percent of the nation's adults say they have never read a book.
- between one in five and one in three Americans are functionally illiterate, depending on the definition of functional illiteracy.
- the U.S. ranks forty-ninth among the 156 United Nations countries in literacy, a drop of eighteen places since 1950.

Against the backdrop of this significant American problem exists a president and a secretary of education who are committed to abolishing the still relatively new Department of Education. It would appear that leadership for the literacy issue will need to come from elsewhere.

Despite the fragmented picture of literacy and the seemingly inadequate approaches to addressing the issue fully, at the individual level many are helped to live more productive and fulfilling lives. In one study sponsored by the New Jersey Basic Skills Assessment Program, results give "ample evidence of the positive impact of the remedial/developmental programs on both retention and academic performance of entering, skills-deficient college students" (Morante, 1986). More studies of this type are needed.

CONCLUSIONS

1. Although there are a great many initiatives on the literacy issues, no national or state-level policy currently exists to provide direction and to focus resources.
2. There are some serious definition problems in discussing the literacy issue.
3. There is a lack of research that focuses on the relevance of assessment to student needs, the relationship of the diagnosis of learn-

ing problems to methodologies being utilized to ameliorate deficiencies, and the outcomes of literacy programs as related to such variables as time-on-task, instructional method, support services provided, and availability of instructional assistance.
4. A real need exists to focus on the politics of illiteracy. It is a "bad breath" issue: almost all are aware of it, a few talk about it, still fewer are willing to confront it.
5. It appears, given the amount of funds available to them, that small and rural colleges are providing a vital service in the literacy area to their communities.
6. Volunteers would appear to be a major untapped resource. Yet, as anyone knows who has worked with volunteers, it is a very time-intensive process. The use of volunteers will require additional funds for coordination and support.
7. The literacy problem is big enough that no one should feel possessive of it. There is enough of the problem to be shared with anyone who desires to help.
8. The literacy problem is not just a public school problem, a community college problem, a four-year college or university problem, or an employer problem; it is a national problem.
9. The shift from an industrial-based to an information/service-based economy is magnifying and will continue to magnify the literacy issue.
10. Some programs are better than others, some approaches yield better results. The identification of exemplary practices can be helpful in improving the quality of literacy programs.
11. Since an increasing percentage of community college enrollment comes from developmental education programs (common for the percentage of the total enrollment to be in the 10-to-30-percent range), accreditation agencies should develop specific standards to evaluate these programs as a way of stimulating improved quality.
12. AACJC and other national organizations should continue to provide national leadership for the literacy issue.

The literacy issue must command a larger share of attention and resources. As David T. Kearns, chairman and chief executive officer of the Xerox Corporation, has said:

Literacy—real literacy—is the essential raw material of the information age. We are entering an era of lifelong learning that merges work and education. Most jobs of the future will be restructured at least once every seven years. By 1990, three out of four jobs will require some education or technical training after high school. (Applebee, Langer, and Mullis 1987)

Even if it were not a requirement for an emerging new society, this issue would still need to be more fully addressed for humane reasons.

BIBLIOGRAPHY

Applebee, Arthur N., Judith A. Langer, and Ina V.S. Mullis. *Learning to Be Literate in America*. Princeton, N.J.: Educational Testing Service, March 1987.

Brier, Ellen. "Bridging the Academic Preparation Gap: An Historical View." *Journal of Developmental Education* 8, No. 1 (1984), pp. 2–5.

Educational Testing Service. *Literacy: Profiles of America's Young Adults*. Report No. 16-PL-02. Princeton, N.J.: ETS, National Assessment of Educational Progress, 1986.

"Functional Literacy and the Workplace." Proceedings of a National Invitational Conference, Educational Services, American Council of Life Insurance, Washington, D.C., 1983.

Morante, Edward A. "The Effectiveness of Developmental Programs: A Two-Year Follow-Up Study." *Journal of Developmental Education* 9, No. 3 (1986).

Platt, Gail M. "Should Colleges Teach Below-College-Level Courses?" *Community College Review* 14, No. 2 (1986), pp. 19–25.

Richardson, Richard C., Elizabeth C. Fisk, and Morris A. Okun. *Literacy in the Open-Access College*. San Francisco: Jossey-Bass, 1983.

Skagen, Anne, ed. *Workplace Literacy*. New York: American Management Association, 1986.

Spann, Milton G., and Cynthia G. Thompson. *The National Directory of Exemplary Programs in Developmental Education*. Boone, N.C.: National Center for Developmental Education, Appalachian State University, 1986.

Treadway, Douglas M. *Higher Education in Rural America*. New York: College Entrance Examination Board, 1984.

Jerry W. Young is superintendent/president of Chaffey College in Rancho-Cucamonga, California.

VI

USES OF TECHNOLOGY

■

By Robert A. Anderson, Jr.

In setting about to determine the use of technology in instruction, support, and administration within small and rural community colleges, a general overview of technology will be described in order to set the stage for the survey that was conducted during 1986/87 by the Commission on Small/Rural Community Colleges as authorized by the American Association of Community and Junior Colleges (AACJC).

In his introduction to *Telelearning Models: Expanding the Community College Community*, James Zigerell quoted from "A Public Trust: The Report of the Carnegie Commission on the Future of Public Broadcasting, 1979," which stated that "technology is advancing so rapidly that it is difficult to predict in what ways it will shape the media. Even now, however, it is clear that with careful planning, skillful execution, and thorough evaluation, telecommunications will play an increasingly fundamental role in the learning processes of Americans of all ages and backgrounds."[1]

It is reasonable to extend that prognostication to all forms of communication technology. John Naisbitt asserts in the first chapter of *Megatrends*, "From an Industrial Society to an Information Society," that today's information technology—from computer to cable television—is a result of a phenomenon that took place in the 1950s: "The years 1956 and 1957 were a turning point, the end of the industrial era.... It is now clear that the post-industrial society is the information society."[2] His conclusion also related to the 1957 launching of the Russian spaceship in which "the real importance of Sputnik is *not* that it began the space age, but that it introduced the era of global satellite communications."[3]

Naisbitt made a prediction, which now appears to have been premature, that teleconferencing would be unsuccessful. In chapter two of *Megatrends*, "Forced Technology—High Tech/High Touch," he stated that teleconferencing "... is another trend that will not happen. Talking with people via television cannot begin to substitute for the high touch of a meeting, no matter how rational it is in saving fuel and overhead.... Teleconferencing is so rational, it will never succeed."[4]

During the fall of 1986 AACJC sponsored its first teleconference, "Community College Partnership: The High School/Community College Connection," which included several hundred community colleges as satellite downlink sites, and in June of 1987 the second national teleconference, focusing on the problem of adult illiteracy in the workplace, was aired, with more than one thousand communities throughout the U.S. involved through downlink sites at community colleges. The third national AACJC-sponsored teleconference, with special emphasis on business and community college partnerships, was presented in September 1987. Additionally, AACJC has contracted with Tradenet/ACCESS, a personal computer-based electronic network, for the purpose of eventually linking all community colleges throughout the country together at a very nominal participation cost in order to facilitate the information exchange flow. Currently, the two major modes of information swap are electronic mail and audioconferencing. The organization providing the nuts-and-bolts leadership in these linkage efforts has been the AACJC-affiliated Instructional Telecommunications Consortium (ITC). Special programs have been sponsored by ITC such as the Annenberg/CPB Project and involvement with the PBS/Adult Learning Service. A proposed Community College Satellite Network is under consideration, with probable adoption in the near future. Maricopa County Community College District Telecommunications has been primary in facilitating the ITC audio conference meetings and more recently the training sessions held for AACJC Board members in bringing on-line the Tradenet/ACCESS system.

National studies have encouraged, even mandated, that education embrace technology as a means of learning transfer as quickly as possible. In fact, the implication has been stressed that public schools, colleges, and universities have a responsibility to provide students with such opportunities in order for them (and the country) to be competitive with other nations in the international setting of political and economic competition.

In a major education reform effort the National Commission on Excellence in Education, in *A Nation at Risk: The Imperative for Educational Reform*, reported that "learning is the indispensable investment required for success in the information age we are entering."[5] The report goes on to say that "these deficiencies come at a time when the demand for highly skilled workers in new fields is accelerating rapidly. For example:

- Computer and computer-controlled equipment are penetrating every aspect of our lives—homes, factories, and offices.
- One estimate indicates that by the turn of the century millions of jobs will involve laser technology and robotics.
- Technology is radically transforming a host of other occupations. They include health care, medical science, energy production, food processing, construction, and the building, repair, and maintenance of sophisticated scientific, educational, military, and industrial equipment."[6]

The report quoted two individuals regarding the paucity of student skills in technology: "Educational researcher Paul Hurd concluded at the end of a thorough national survey of student achievement that within the context of the modern scientific revolution, 'we are raising a new generation of Americans that is scientifically and technologically illiterate.' In a similar vein, John Slaughter, a former director of the National Science Foundation, warned of 'a growing chasm between a small scientific and technological elite and a citizenry ill-formed, indeed uninformed, on issues with a science component!'"[7] The report asserts that "knowledge of the humanities... must be harnessed to science and technology if the latter are to remain creative and humane, just as the humanities need to be informed by science and technology if they are too relevant to the human condition."[8]

A later Carnegie special report by Frank Newman, *Higher Education and the American Resurgence*, stated that "the most commonly expressed concern about higher education over the last several years is that it may not graduate enough engineers and computer scientists to meet the demands of the new high technology economy."[9] In chapter nine of the same report, it is suggested that "the ability of the U.S. to compete economically and politically depends not only on research leadership, but also on leadership in developing technology, and its capacity to turn that technology into imaginative new products.... The universities' ability to translate into technology and the effectiveness of the linkages between universities and industry are, however, of major concern to us."[10]

The implications for community colleges are very direct and of great magnitude. Dale Parnell, president of AACJC, in describing issues to be addressed in cultivating excellence in education, cited those of technological tension, educational tension, and socioeconomic tension. Regarding technological tensions, Parnell states, "Our society grows technically and scientifically more sophisticated, yet continues to produce an increasing number of individuals who are uneducated, unskilled, and unable to cope with these technological changes."[11]

The continuing rapid expansion of technological advances presents certain frustration for those expected to provide a learning setting reflective of the latest state-of-the-art technological devices that are applicable to educational processes. However, great strides have been made—both philosophically and practically—in the acquisition of such devices and the adaptation by human resources to an educational environment that is literally being forced to effect changes as a response to emerging technologies. There has been a general response by community colleges throughout the nation to become role models in technology use, in providing technology transfer to students, and in cooperating with business and industry in creating special training programs for employees. Small and rural community colleges haven't missed a beat in responding to the demands to enter into the arena of technology.

DESCRIPTION OF SURVEY INSTRUMENT

The survey instrument developed to elicit responses included a two-page section that listed a variety of technologies, with the instruction to identify those being utilized at the institution and to comment briefly about how the technology was applied both in instructional programs and in administrative support. There were three major technologies categories—computer, telecommunications, and radio—each with a number of subsets.

Over half of the 1,230 community, technical, and junior colleges fall within the parameters describing small and/or rural colleges, namely, less than 2,000 FTE and/or in a rural setting. Approximately six hundred institutions with eight hundred campuses fall within one or both of the categories. Surveys were sent to 568 of the colleges, of which 228 returned completed instruments for a return rate of 40 percent.

STATES REPRESENTED IN THE SURVEY

Most states were represented by institutions responding to the survey form: Alabama, 5; Alaska, 3; Arizona, 6; Arkansas, 6; California, 16; Colorado, 4; Connecticut, 4; Florida, 2; Georgia, 4; Hawaii, 1; Idaho, 2; Illinois, 13; Iowa, 5; Kansas, 13; Kentucky, 3; Louisiana, 1; Maine, 1; Maryland, 5; Massachusetts, 2; Michigan, 3; Minnesota, 6; Mississippi, 6; Missouri, 2; Montana, 2; Nebraska, 5; New Hampshire, 1; New Jersey, 1; New Mexico, 7; New York, 8; North Carolina, 21; North Dakota, 5; Ohio, 12; Oklahoma, 3; Oregon, 4; Pennsylvania, 4; South Carolina, 9; South Dakota, 1; Tennessee, 6; Texas, 6; Vermont, 1; Virginia, 9; Washington, 4; West Virginia, 1; Wisconsin, 1; and Wyoming, 4.

COMPOSITE RESPONSE ANALYSIS

It may be stated at the outset that the questionnaires returned should not be construed as being totally representative of small and rural community colleges. There were a number of institutions known to incorporate the utilization of technologies for instruction and administration support that did not return the survey instrument. However, those that were returned indicate a rather high degree of technologies utilization, the predominant area being computers, some form of telecommunication next, and radio the least.

Regarding use of computers, 195 of the 228 respondents reported some type of computer-aided or -assisted instruction, 125 incorporated computer-aided design in their curriculum, and 177 institutions utilized computers in their administrative support system.

The telecommunications section incorporated the most questions, with subcategories under the headings of college television station, public television broadcasting system, commercial television, satellite, and special services. Under college television station, forty-eight reported having or utilizing cable TV, twenty-eight employed the use of a one-way station, thirteen had VHF stations, seven had UHF, eleven had developed ITFS systems, eleven had two-way systems, and four were using low-power stations.

Forty-nine of the 228 colleges employed use of a public television broadcasting system, while thirty-four incorporated commercial television. In conjunction with use of satellite transmission, seventy-five reported downlink capabilities and six stated that they had the capability to up-link broadcasts.

Special services included electronic blackboard, which thirteen schools reported having. Twenty-one have microwave capability, eight have installed a fiber-optic system, seven-two have been involved in teleconferencing, and five have slow-scan systems.

Under radio technology the categories were FM station, AM station, commercial station, and public broadcast station. Twenty institutions reporting having FM stations, three of which had an AM station and eight of which were undesignated. Of those, sixteen were classified as commercial stations and fifteen as public broadcasting stations.

Two other general questions were asked the respondents: one dealing with use of the telephone for audio counseling and the other with participation in a consortium with other agencies relative to the use of technology. In the former, twenty-seven colleges stated they had specific audio counseling programs vis-à-vis telephone, and the latter question elicited a response from fifty-six institutions indicating formal membership in a consortium that had as a major purpose the use or advancement of technology with direct relationship to instruction or administrative support.

EXEMPLARY USE/APPLICATION OF TECHNOLOGY BY INSTITUTIONS

Some of the respondents described in various detail the utilization of technology at their institutions. Predicated on those descriptions, several are cited in the following paragraphs as being noteworthy.

Northwest Community College in Alaska shares courses and technology with *Chukchi Community College* and *Kuskokwin Community College* as part of a state-system consortium. Additionally, Northwest has a one-way cable television VHF station along with satellite downlink capabilities. Slow scan, teleconferencing, and the development of the electronic blackboard are also available. Audio capabilities include use of a commercial station and telephone conferencing. *Kenai Peninsula Community College* and *Ketchikan Community College* reported similar technological capabilities. An extensive statewide computer system is available for support as well.

Garland County Community College, Arkansas, reported use of a closed-circuit television system on campus as well as offering telecollege courses for credit in conjunction with the Arkansas Educational Television Network. *Southern Arkansas University Tech* has created a brochure titled "Opening Doors in Computer-Aided Technology." *Islands Com-*

munity College stated that Arkansas has an extensive statewide computer system for administrative support in which they participate.

Arizona Western College has an AM radio station, used for instructional purposes, which also functions as a public broadcasting station. *South Mountain Community College* has implemented an electronic mail and word-processing service for its staff, which is used daily. *Northland Pioneer College*, a decentralized institution that has no main campus, is installing a two-way video system at nine locations in an initial phase to support an instructional program that covers a geographic area one hundred miles wide by almost three hundred miles long and includes three Indian reservations.

College of the Siskiyous in California has a closed-circuit, one-way television system that is transmitted to twenty-five classrooms on campus plus a receive-only ITFS system whereby upper-division classes are received via microwave linkage with California State University at Chico. *Columbia College* is a member of the Higher Education Consortium of Central California, which also includes *Merced Community College, Modesto Community College, San Joaquin Delta Community College,* and an ITFS linkage with Stanislaus State University. *Crafton Hills Community College* indicated that its district provides the local Public Broadcasting Service System, and *Gavilan College* has both an ITFS microwave system and commercial cable television capabilities. *Mt. San Jacinto College* reported housing a commercial radio station. *Sierra College* has receive-and-send capabilities over a dedicated cable television channel that is used for both prerecorded and live video classes. At *Taft College* over 50 percent of the faculty use a computer in one or more aspects of instructional strategies, with 90 percent of the faculty being computer literate. Additionally, it operates a PBS cable television station twenty-four hours a day, seven days a week. *Victor Valley College*, which uses the local PBS as well as other commercial television stations to offer credit courses, belongs to the Southern California Consortium for Community College Television. *Yuba Community College District* reported belonging to a regional television consortium as well.

Northeastern Junior College of Colorado cooperates with KRMA-TV in Denver to provide telecourses for college credit, and states that high school counselors throughout the state have access to a toll-free 800 telephone number to talk with admission and counseling personnel at the institution.

Mohegan Community College indicated that it uses the Connecticut state computer system for administrative support and *Quinebaug Valley Community College* stated that the Connecticut Community College System has a public television broadcasting system.

Lake City Community College, Florida, in addition to downlink, has uplink capabilities with its satellite television equipment. The college also provides an ITFS system plus VHF cable.

Bainbridge Junior College on occasion does teleconferencing with other units of the University System of Georgia. Also, Georgia Public TV is sometimes used to support humanities and political science classes in its curriculum.

College of Southern Idaho relies on its public television broadcasting system and cable television in its curriculum delivery, and *North Idaho College* utilizes KSPS public television out of Spokane, Washington, which is approximately twenty miles across the state line, to broadcast its telecourses, in addition to its local cable television station in Coeur d'Alene, where the college is located.

Robert Morris College in Illinois is a member of CONVOCOM, a regional, jointly operated PBS television station comprising members from both secondary and postsecondary education and the business/industry sector. *John Wood Community College* is likewise a member of CONVOCOM. It offers several courses over the local PBS network as a member facility and is currently installing a two-way microwave with that entity.

Iowa Lakes Community College reported that teleconferencing occurs among fifteen Iowa community colleges. There is a two-way microwave between its own campuses and an ITFS system in a five-county area, including six current sites, with twenty local schools to be added by 1988. Seventy percent of all programs at the institution have computers in their instructional delivery system. *North Iowa Area Community College* has two teleconferencing sites in its service area, which is part of a statewide network used for administrative functions and increasing instructional purposes. *Northeast Iowa Technical Institute* has a downlink satellite receiver at two centers with large-screen projection. It is a member of NUTN, which allows national teleconferencing. Additionally, the institute reported that the Iowa area community colleges have a statewide audio conferencing system used for programming as well as general meetings.

Seward County Community College is a member of KAPSET, the Kansas Association for Post Secondary Educational Television, which is an organization to promote and organize telecourses for colleges and universities throughout the state. It also uses ADVONET, which is an electronic mail system between the state department of education and the Kansas community colleges. *Pratt Community College* is also a member of KAPSET and uses the PBS system to offer one to two courses each semester as a member of the state telecourse consortium. Special services capabilities reported include an electronic blackboard tied to the state office and teleconferencing over a dedicated line as part of a statewide network. *Hutchinson Community College* uses the same special services. *Colby Community College* develops the program for a channel on the local cable television station as part of its television production program, and *Labette Community College* provides classes at eight sites over cable television.

Allegany Community College in Maryland broadcasts over a local access channel of a cable television station a program called *ACC Byline*. Local cable reception is fed to each teaching area on campus, plus there are three separate channels to the same areas via a closed-circuit system.

The institution has an extensive system of personal computer labs, each dedicated to Apple, IBM, NCR, and mainframe network terminals. *Harford Community College* has an FM radio station as well as a local access public television station.

Mount Wachusett Community College and *Greenfield Community College* in Massachusetts have college radio stations (the former is in-house only). Mount Wachusett indicated use of cable television, having satellite downlink capabilities, and special services of electronic blackboard, microwave, teleconferencing, and slow-scan television. Greenfield operates a college television station that is one-way, two-way, and has cable television access.

University of Minnesota Technical College, Crookston has five personal computer labs on campus with about 25 percent of the faculty using PCs in their offices. Over 50 percent of its full-time faculty (55) will have office PCs by fall 1987. *Northeast Metro Technical Institute* reported having satellite television downlink and uplink capabilities for its teleconferencing.

Copiah-Lincoln Junior College is a member of the Mississippi Educational Television Council for Higher Education and through that broadcasting entity periodically offers credit courses. It also has a college-owned and student-run FM, noncommercial radio station. Two courses of communication credit are available for on-the-air lab experience. *East Central Junior College* cited ITFS and cable television capabilities, using both UHF and VHF frequencies.

Salish Kootenai College in Montana is developing a low-power television station for implementation in fall 1987. It currently has a satellite dish for receiving purposes and tape programs for instructional use.

McCook Community College and *Mid-Plains Technical Community College Area* in Nebraska have downlink satellite capabilities, use cable television for instruction (the latter ABE and GED classes via the system), and have a slow-scan college television station used for teaching off-campus courses.

The *Dona Ana Branch Community College–New Mexico State University* utilizes the parent institution's FM radio station and television station. *Eastern New Mexico University–Roswell Branch* is a member of the National University Teleconferencing Network (NUTN) and is linked by a microwave ITFS system with the parent institution. *Santa Fe Community College*, which has been in existence just four years, plans an FM radio station for the summer of 1988, with FCC licensing already secured. A telecommunications coordinator has been hired to develop programs and design facilities as part of its new $15 million campus, which has just commenced construction. Currently, telecourses are being offered over commercial cable TV. *San Juan College*, which has just constructed a new computer technology building, offers telecourses and public service programming of speakers on and off campus, provides classical music over the VHF cable television channel, and facilitates teleconferencing for public schools, businesses, and other agencies. The *University of New Mexico–Los Alamos Campus* shares part of its facilities with the Los Alamos National Laboratory Training Center, which in turn allows the institution access to special services, including electronic blackboard, microwave, fiber optic, teleconferencing, and slow scan. *New Mexico Junior College* participates in a telecommunications consortium with Eastern New Mexico University through a microwave, two-way ITFS system, which also allows access to linkage with the University of New Mexico, New Mexico State University, and the state capitol. Over seventy videotapes are produced in the institutional television studio each year to supplement instructional courses. The college has an in-house system with one-way receive drops to nineteen classrooms; there are two satellite dishes mounted on top of the library/IRC, which allows receipt of five channels for direct broadcast or taping; and institutional/commercial educational programming is provided to two cable television stations twenty hours a day, seven days a week. NMJC has the largest telecollege enrollment of any of the twenty-three public colleges and universities in the state. A telecommunications system is currently under design that will eventually link the institution with five public school systems, a small private four-year college, and all county libraries, municipalities, and government offices. A dedicated computer line links the college's area vocational high school, located on campus, to one of the participating public high schools for the purpose of reporting daily attendance of students on released time. Also, a telephone line from the college's public information office has been dedicated to one of the local daily newspapers for the purpose of computer-generated news releases.

Adirondack Community College in New York has an FM radio station as well as a television studio that is primarily used for production of videotaped material in support of classes. *Columbia-Greene Community College* has an FM radio station and has just begun a microwave partnership with area high schools. *Niagara County Community College* has developed an interactive videodisc for noncredit course offerings in business planning. A tourism training disc has been written, edited, and produced on campus, with business and tourism discs implemented on a statewide basis. *Sullivan County Community College* has a one-way college television station used for instruction and registration, along with use of VHF cable television station broadcast. Fiber-optic special services are being used in a research capacity. *Morrisville Agricultural and Technical College*, which is part of the SUNY system, includes a student-operated radio system on its cable network as part of the journalism curriculum. It describes an extensive computer-related operation from faculty-developed CAI to a computer-aided tutorial program for remediation. The campus has a closed-circuit cable system over which educational programs from three satellite receive dishes are transmitted to classrooms and dormitories, as well as access twenty-four hours a day to the institutional two-way computer and broadcast systems. An example is extensive use of the electronic blackboard for messages between students and faculty. *Ulster County Community College* has an AM radio station for on-campus use only and produces four hours per week of programming over its local cablevision station.

Carteret Technical College provides satellite uplink telecommunications with the North Carolina Department of Community Colleges and plans in the near future both C- and Ku-band downlinks. Teleconferencing as a receive site has occurred with NUTN and PBS. Cable television programming is transmitted to its main classroom building. *Lenoir Community College* is likewise involved with teleconferencing through the North Carolina Department of Community Colleges and provides courses through public television. It also has a 3,000-watt FM radio station in operation. *Western Piedmont Community College* is a member of the community college consortium on Professional Competencies and Technological Training, and *Wilkes Community College* is a member of NUTN and the North Carolina Public Broadcasting System. Its FM radio station provides training in the radio-television broadcasting curriculum along with distribution of programs from satellite and cable transmission throughout the campus. The college has two C-band TVRO systems and soon plans to acquire a KU-band TVRO.

Bismarck State Community College provided a statement that all eleven colleges and universities in North Dakota are hooked into a multimillion-dollar state higher education system that "has more capacity, power, and service than we know how to use."

Belmont Technical College stated that all two-year colleges in Ohio are computer-linked for communications. *Central Ohio Technical College* has a two-way link to broadcast facilities of a local cablevision company. *Ohio University/Belmont* has just installed a new FM radio station for local instruction and community service. It shares a PBS television station with the main campus, with recent implementation of two-way microwave capability among the Ohio University regional campuses for instructional and administrative purposes. *Rio Grande Community College* reported a campus television station with one-way capability.

El Reno Junior College, Northeastern Oklahoma A and M College, and *Seminole Junior College* in Oklahoma all use the public television broadcasting system to offer courses. Seminole has talk-back television capability for classes and special meetings.

Blue Mountain Community College of Oregon has a campus FM radio station and satellite downlink facilities for programs offered on campus. *Tillamook Bay Community College* is affiliated with the Oregon Telecommunications Consortium and the Oregon Public Broadcasting System.

Lehigh County Community College, Pennsylvania, uses its one-way college television station for video bulletins, alerting students about developmental resources.

Anderson College in South Carolina utilizes a channel on the local cable television for use by its journalism department. *Horry-Georgetown*

Technical College, Florence Darlington Technical College, Piedmont Technical College, and *Spartanburg Technical College* are all linked to the closed-circuit South Carolina Educational Television System for teleconferencing and instructional purposes. Piedmont is developing plans to deliver instruction to off-campus sites via microwave. *Sumter Area Technical College* facilitates conferences for state and local agencies (e.g., Fire Chief, State Developmental Board projects) and voting personnel utilizing the public television broadcasting system. *York Technical College* has implemented microwave and fiber-optic special services along with a two-way ITFS college television station that is being phased in. Additionally, it has both down- and uplink capabilities.

Roane State Community College in Tennessee uses a writing center hotline via telephone on its two campuses. Four in-house television channels are available for the CCTV network from its media center to classrooms and labs. The college's satellite downlink facilities have been used for several teleconferences, with special NASA broadcasts beamed to its classrooms. The Local Area Network for data transmission is now under development to utilize fiber-optic and coax cable. *Walters State Community College* teaches a number of courses via public television, and it has its own college television studio as part of a closed-circuit system throughout the campus.

Frank Phillips College, Texas, reports having spent $100,000 on computer-assisted instruction over the past three years. It has just constructed a public broadcast television station and began offering classes to three off-campus locations by microwave. *Laredo Junior College* is currently constructing a one-way cable television station.

New River Community College in Virginia receives programs on TVRO for use in classrooms on a per-individual-request basis. It operates a one-way campus television channel, as part of the CCTV, for instructional and entertainment programming. The college plans to access a channel through its local cable television company, and currently receives NCTV, the Learning Channel, and teleconferencing over its downlink satellite equipment. *Virginia Highlands Community College* has both VHF and UHF television along with both down- and uplink satellite capabilities. *Wytheville Community College* is linked to the Virginia Community College System computer mainframe, which provides administrative support for scheduling, admissions, registration, inventory, financial aid, research, and business office reports.

Olympic College in Washington is a member of the Puget Sound Center for Telecommunications. The college uses the public television broadcasting system for offering telecourses. *Skagit Valley College* has an FM public broadcast radio station on campus and uses commercial television via satellite to offer selected courses.

Southern West Virginia Community College is reaching 90 percent of the service area population with its programming over a cable television channel and is in the process of hooking up in a second county. It has two satellite dishes (Harris System) on two main campuses over which the college programs C-span and the campus network. The college also has uplink capabilities and uses audio teleconferencing between campuses and centers in its service area of four counties.

District One Technical Institute is a member of the TAE Media Consortium, which encompasses sixteen districts throughout the state of Wisconsin. The institute also belongs to the Indian Head Higher Education Media Consortium, which is a regional grouping of four universities and two technical institutes. The institute is planning to implement a one-way ITFS college television system in 1988 and currently operates a twelve-channel CCTV system with a distribution to over fourteen thousand a year. General and credit courses are provided to three cities. Two twelve-foot satellite receiving dishes pull in approximately one hundred fifty programs.

Central Wyoming College has a college FM radio station and owns its PBS television station. Its television capabilities include one-way, VHF cable, and low power. The college has both down- and uplink capabilities along with microwave. *Laramie County Community College* has one-way, VHF cable television capability. *Sheridan College* is a member of the Wyoming Higher Education Computer Network, which was created to prevent duplication of equipment, software, and staff among area colleges, provide computer maintenance and support, as well as share resources with the University of Wyoming. The college uses cable television for production and enhancement of programming for the student body relative to entertainment, news, and general information. The system is used to communicate to the community at large and for teleconferencing. *Western Wyoming Community College* is building an ITFS television system that will include electronic blackboard, fiber-optic, slow-scan, and teleconferencing capabilities.

CONCLUSIONS AND PREDICTIONS ABOUT FUTURE USE OF TECHNOLOGIES

It is obvious that most small and rural community colleges have incorporated the use of technology in their institutional operations. The predominant use was computer support for administrative reporting and instructional purposes. Thirty-one of the 228 respondents had radio stations, and 28 had television systems ranging from transmission of local cable company programming to very elaborate microwave, two-way ITFS systems including uplink satellite broadcasting capability. Many of the institutions make use of television programming, although they do not have station or system facilities.

Several states have implemented computer support systems, primarily for administrative reporting purposes, but there is evidence that some computer-aided instruction support is available. Telecommunications in the form of microwave, cable, and instructional television fixed service (ITFS) is in evidence on a regionalized consortium basis as well as to some degree throughout state systems. It is especially evident among those states that, on the one hand, have a large number of community colleges, so that reporting logistics are abbreviated, and states that have few institutions or populations dispersed in large geographic service areas, which emphasizes the need for incorporating instructional and administrative support delivery systems.

The future use of technology will obviously be of greater magnitude as institutions, state agencies, and educational organizations become more skilled in its use and application, as well as feel more comfortable as it becomes commonplace in everyday functions. It appears that computer support for administrative functions has become a necessity, while support for computer-aided instructional programs and activities will have ever-increasing focus, especially as philosophical discussions occur regarding acceptability of methodology. The recent decision by AACJC to provide a computer linkage system to be accessed by all two-year institutions is a major step in shrinking former distance barriers for information sharing as well as in implementing the ultimate "one voice" concept in national alert matters of legislative significance.

Telecommunications will continue to be an area of prominence and will most assuredly accelerate. National conferences emanating from AACJC offices is of signal importance inasmuch as virtually any institution may purchase or rent a receiving device at very low cost with the telephone as audio connector. Ultimately, origination capabilities will also be cost-effective so that time and distance factors will be abated. Satellite "birds," owned or time-leased, will become even more sophisticated but will also be in greater demand. "Space" in space may be a crucial problem in the future.

Linkages and partnerships among community colleges and, likewise, between community colleges and other entities—school districts, universities, state and federal agencies, business and industry, municipalities, county and state government offices, libraries, media, individuals—are natural spinoffs. Collaboration and cooperation, however, may be challenged by fiscal competitiveness and the need for certain independence.

Overall, technology and technology transfer will continue to be high profile. Like most anything else, the combination of futurism and practical application suggests many interesting years to come as efforts are made to provide greater service to our students and public.

NOTES

[1] James Zigerell, *Telelearning Models: Expanding the Community College Community*, Community College Issues Series No. 3 (Washington, D.C.: American Association of Community and Junior Colleges, 1986), p. vii.

[2] John Naisbitt, *Megatrends—Ten New Directions Transforming Our Lives* (New York: Warner, 1982), p. 13.

[3]Ibid., p. 12.
[4]Ibid., p. 46.
[5]National Commission on Excellence in Education, *A Nation at Risk: The Imperative for Educational Reform* (Washington, D.C.: GPO, 1983), p. 7.
[6]Ibid., p. 10.
[7]Ibid.
[8]Ibid, pp. 10–11.
[9]Frank Newman, *Higher Education and the American Resurgence* (Princeton, N.J.: Carnegie Foundation for the Advancement of Teaching, 1985), p. 43.
[10]Ibid., p. 112.
[11]Dale Parnell, *The Neglected Majority* (Washington, D.C.: Community College Press, 1985), p. 21.

Robert A. Anderson, Jr. is president of New Mexico Junior College in Hobbs, New Mexico.

VII

Resource Development

By Judson H. Flower

Resource development—the ofttimes mystifying pursuit of external dollars—creates something of a dilemma for the small/rural community college. The quest for external funding support is a roller-coaster ride of ups and downs for any institution. The smaller the institution and its budget, the more these variations are magnified. The degree of positive impact and the resulting "high" that comes from a successful federal program application or a foundation grant is enlarged because of its greater relative proportion to the operations of a small institution.

Conversely, the "low" that flows from an unsuccessful grant application, following long and laborious effort, can have a substantial negative potential. Worse yet is the devastating impact of the discontinuance or severe reduction of valued programs or services attending the loss or expiration of an external funding source. Almost always this is the result of inadequate planning, which should have assured an improved programmatic product and a smooth transition to a traditional revenue base.

Best of all is the happy experience when a thoroughly planned developmental undertaking intersects with the purposes and priorities of an external funding source. A well-prepared application receives agency or foundation approval; planned activities are implemented with the full support and enthusiasm of an involved faculty and staff; and a developmental program is firmly established, with provision for its continuance beyond the period of external funding assistance. The uplift is palpable, and lays a solid foundation for the next developmental phase.

Data that would help define the extent to which small and rural colleges are engaged in resource development are not readily available. AACJC interprets *small* and *rural* to encompass institutions that are small *and/or* rural. Small includes colleges under 2,000 FTE (full-time enrollment), but there is no uniform definition of rural. Any institution may call itself rural simply by choosing to do so, regardless of its location or proximity to large population centers. As a result, there are many so-called rural colleges with enrollments substantially higher than 2,000 FTE, grouped together with much smaller institutions, which effectively prevents the gathering of truly comparable data.

Even without precise data, there are clear indications that small, geographically isolated two-year colleges are significantly less involved in resource development than their larger urban counterparts. This is partly due to limitations of budget resources and staff personnel; but perceptions, attitudes, and commitment toward resource development are also highly important factors. Primary attention is herein focused upon resource development in those colleges that are both small *and* rural.

The most essential ingredient in a successful resource development program is the harmonious meshing of resource development efforts with the realities of institutional needs. Few approaches are more futile, or potentially injurious, than merely seeking dollars for dollars' sake.

An accurate needs assessment must be undertaken, with careful attention to process and analysis, so that a proper identification of developmental needs is assured. Faculty and staff across the broad range of instructional programs and institutional operations must be actively involved throughout the needs assessment process. An appropriate variety of community representatives must be similarly involved. This should actually be easier to accomplish in a smaller institution because the numbers of persons and programs to be incorporated into the process are fewer than in larger institutions.

A close cooperation among faculty and staff throughout a small/rural institution is essential for the successful implementation of any developmental program. Individuals who have not been consulted or otherwise actively involved during the needs assessment and planning phases will not look kindly upon the roles expected of them during the program implementation phase. A certain amount of not being involved in everything is expected, or at least tolerated, in larger institutions. However, unhappiness and noncooperation among a disgruntled few can raise havoc in the close environment of a small institution.

The Title III "Developing Institutions" model, cumbersome and tedious as it may be, is a sound approach to the long-range planning process that underlies a solid resource development program. The detailed procedures for matching the goals, objectives, and activities of any specific developmental undertaking against the priorities of an institutional long-range plan is in itself a highly productive process, and goes a long way toward assuring the successful outcome of resource development efforts.

A common pitfall for resource development efforts in the small/rural college is the too frequent assumption that the task can not be managed because of limitations of budget, staff size, and available expertise. Hence no central focus or responsibility is established, and in its place a piecemeal effort at resource development is made with fragmented bits of time and personnel.

A certain route to failure is to assign all faculty and staff members to fit resource development into their schedules whenever a little time can be spared from their major functional roles and responsibilities. Few ever find time to do anything at all. Those who manage to do something rarely move beyond minimal accomplishment. Effective planning and coordination among those making an effort at resource development are rendered impotent.

Underlying every truly successful program of resource development is a total commitment by the college president and governing board. This commitment is reflected not only in the assignment of staff and the allocation of budget resources, but in the personal dedication and active involvement of the president.

If for no other reason than smallness of staff to whom tasks can be delegated, the president of a small/rural college must accept a greater personal role in resource development. In all institutions there are certain functions in the process of raising external funds that are best accomplished by the president. This is not a result of greater expertise, talent, or strength of personality. It is simply a reflection that the position of president carries a clearly identified focus and prestige to which those at the giving/granting end of the resource development spectrum gravitate.

To some extent this is unfair to those who actually perform most of the grassroots functions of resource development, but it is a fact that is generally accepted without complaint. There is no excuse for the president who is unprepared or unqualified for his or her role and as a result fails to carry off the prize at the critical moment. This threat requires the president of the small/rural college to be more knowledgeable and capable in the inner workings and processes of resource development, simply because he or she does not have a cadre of subordinate experts upon whom he or she can depend. The smaller the institution, the more significant and direct the personal role of the president.

Still, even in the smallest of institutions, the president can not accomplish the goals of resource development alone. Some presidents may be very successful in attracting donor contributions to the college. However, to be able to raise dollars by dint of personal persuasion and effort is to miss the point. To really accomplish the aims of resource development—to bring growth and improvement to the broad spectrum of institutional programs and operations—requires the involvement of many individuals.

The small/rural college, despite its lack of personnel and financial resources, must nonetheless be prepared to commit a significant portion of budget funds to the function of resource development. These budget resources must include an allocation of the dollars essential to establish a resource development office, with personnel, staff, and/or secretarial assistance; office space and related equipment; and an operational budget adequate to provide for supplies, travel, and training.

The size of the resource development office may vary considerably from one institution to another, and smaller institutions have been very successful with less than full-time personnel. However, any part-time approach must be sufficient that specific roles are assigned, and that substantial time and budgetary resources are dedicated to the task.

It is of vital importance that someone be designated the function of development officer. Full-time is highly preferable, but circumstances may not allow more than a part-time role. The critical factor is that someone have specific responsibility for carrying out the resource development function. Administrators, faculty, and staff must know who that individual is, and be expected to have an active working relationship in which they can initiate ideas of their own and/or respond to suggestions and ideas presented by the development officer.

It is also of extreme importance that the person designated to the role of development officer have regular and ready access to the administrative circles where institutional planning takes place. Whether technically a member of the administrative staff or not, the development officer should be generally considered as such, and should attend and participate actively in administrative meetings and planning sessions. Only in this way can the development officer have a ready awareness of the directions in which program areas, departments, divisions, and the institution itself are moving.

Through a knowledge of these directions, the development officer can use his or her expertise to develop a linkage with external funding sources that might provide the badly needed revenues to make growth and development possible. It then becomes necessary to activate the previously established interrelationships among faculty and staff, individually or in appropriate groupings, to move toward the detailed planning that leads to the inquiries and formal applications that will hopefully result in the desired funding assistance.

A broad variable in the resource development efforts of small and rural colleges is the degree to which those individuals assigned to the function of resource development possess the depth and sweep of expertise essential to the task. The list of functional areas is formidable, and includes:

- Federal and state agency programs;
- Grants management and program accountability;
- Private and corporate foundations;
- Institutional foundations/endowments;
- Personal giving, bequests, trusts;
- Alumni associations;
- Special projects, capital construction;
- Annual giving campaigns (letter and telephone); and
- Management of development office staff and operations.

Federal and state agency programs run the gamut of college instructional and operational activities, and require an understanding of the peculiarities of myriads of governmental agencies. Private and corporate foundations are only moderately less complex. Community college foundations are a fairly recent phenomenon, especially in small/rural institutions. Personal giving, bequests, trusts, etc., require an exacting legal understanding and in-depth knowledge of estate and tax laws. Alumni associations require an immense flow of mail and paperwork to keep track of graduates and former students who are forever on the move. Special projects and capital construction take on a life of their own that can become time consuming in awesome proportion. Fundraising by letter and telephone campaigns, unless exceptionally well done, generally produces a rather low yield in comparison with effort expended. While these obstacles present a distinct challenge, they can be overcome and should not preclude the small/rural college from undertaking an active program on resource development.

It is rare that a small/rural community college would have a resource development staff possessed of expertise in all of the above areas. Further, it is not likely that smaller institutions would be actively engaged in all of these development functions. It is far more probable that expertise will have to be developed in-house over a period of time as the college ventures into new facets of resource development. This will require specific training of the development office staff.

There are numerous organizations that provide training for resource development personnel. Each has particular strengths that, through careful selection, can add to the capabilities of a small/rural college development office staff. However, the National Council for Resource Development (NCRD), one of the affiliate councils of AACJC, is the single best source of comprehensive training for those engaged in resource development in the small/rural college. NCRD, comprising more than nine hundred members, is the only organization devoted solely to the training of resource development professionals in two-year, community, technical, and junior colleges across the nation.

NCRD holds a national conference in Washington, D.C., each December to train and inform in the multiresponsibilities and functions of resource development personnel. Many of the sessions of this conference are appropriate to the particular needs of small and rural colleges. Regional NCRD conferences are also held across the country, providing similar training opportunities. In addition, NCRD maintains a full-time office in the AACJC suite in Washington, D.C., where information is readily available to assist small and rural colleges in their resource development efforts.

Resource development at any level is not an enterprise for the faint of heart. Small and rural community colleges have much to gain from a well-planned and implemented resource development program. Not to venture is to lose the game before it has started. With proper thought and careful planning there is no need to fear being overwhelmed. Go for it!

Judson H. Flower is president of Miles Community College in Miles City, Montana.

VIII

COMMITMENT TO ACCESS

By John E. Pickelman and Marc A. Nigliazzo

No concept has been more integral to the community college in America than that of open access. It is, simply, a firm belief that all individuals who seek the opportunities afforded by this unique institution of higher education should have access to those opportunities, and that it is incumbent upon the community college in fulfilling its mission to facilitate that access. And, probably, no aspect of its mission has been more fervently pursued. Unfortunately, no aspect of its mission has brought the community college in America more criticism than that very pursuit. The community college has sometimes been accused in the 1980s of so completely committing itself to student access that it has occasionally forsaken student progress, creating as a consequence the concept of the revolving door, admitting many but leaving many unfulfilled, never having achieved the opportunity promised.

However, the results of a 1987 AACJC survey of small and rural community colleges lend credibility to the original belief that access can produce opportunity, and that the community college in America has withstood the criticism and redoubled its efforts to ensure a balance between the two. What follows is a summary of the survey's findings. It is a synthesis of more than two hundred responses from across America, from community colleges and technical institutes ranging in size from a few hundred to several thousand students and serving constituencies of approximately ten thousand to more than three hundred thousand (most serve fewer than three thousand students with a constituency of fewer than one hundred thousand). All of the reporting colleges are essentially rural in nature, ranging in location from the plains of west Texas to the Appalachians, from the farmlands of the Midwest to isolated communities in the Alaskan mountains.

Much of what is demonstrated by these small and rural community colleges parallels all community colleges, but the unique approaches required to reach a scattered and sometimes isolated constituency—sometimes a reluctant constituency—show through. In total, the survey demonstrates an unwavering commitment to both access and opportunity, and affirms the ability of the community college to achieve both. In summarizing the results of the survey, we have stressed the efforts made by rural community colleges to recruit students and to provide transition into the college setting, but we have also explored their efforts to assure progress toward opportunity once the student is within the door.

RECRUITMENT

Within the complete spectrum of access with opportunity, the community college faces always the challenge of recruiting prospective students, making them aware of the opportunities available and encouraging their pursuit of those opportunities. The trend most consistently evolving is the development of a marketing plan, a blueprint for recruitment activities. Many community colleges, and a surprisingly large number of the small and rural community colleges, have committed themselves not only to a comprehensive marketing plan but to the hiring of one or more full-time recruiters to implement the plan. The plan itself usually provides a detailed outline of recruiting activities with dates, costs, and responsible personnel. Counselors, admissions officers, faculty committees, and, increasingly, professional recruiters coordinate implementation.

Recruitment activities vary with individual colleges and their locations, but there is the usual array of traditional recruiting approaches including extensive use of media (radio, television, and print media) along with some new twists on the use of billboards (especially electronic ones), bumper stickers, pamphlets, newsletters, and posters. The mass mailing of recruitment information remains ever-popular, especially the mailing of schedules, as do other traditional measures such as information booths at shopping malls, open houses, testimonials from prominent graduates, and letters to graduating seniors. The phoning of prospective students (including actual phonathons) is becoming more popular. And almost all colleges reporting in the survey indicated the targeting of special populations. For instance, one community college holds a special luncheon each year for honor graduates of area high schools. Others have made a practice of recruiting from National Guard armories. And, of course, many use adult reentry projects.

Of the more unique efforts at recruiting, one community college decrees a Community Day during which all college employees are dispersed into the community to make known the availability of college programs. Another college has begun to use student ambassadors, college students selected and trained to enter area high schools for the purpose of recruitment. To offset large but sparsely populated service areas, several small and rural community colleges have begun to mail videotapes to prospective students upon request. While yet another community college has purchased and equipped a mobile registration trailer to travel physically the breadth of its service area. In all of these cases, the purpose is to get the word out and to encourage participation.

Supporting direct recruitment is the ongoing effort by most small and rural community colleges to maintain visibility and to thus ensure that the service population does not forget the presence of the college. Encouraging college personnel to participate in speakers' bureaus and to be active members of community organizations seems to be the common approach, as does the reliance upon college cultural or athletic events to focus positive attention on college resources. College days for high school students are used extensively, with the most effective reported to be those held on the college campus. In fact, the desirability of getting prospective students on campus was often stressed in the survey responses and is achieved in a range of other activities from adult reentry seminars to cultural festivals and scholastic contests. In all of the events, maintenance of visibility is an indirect but key support of recruitment.

TRANSITION

As students become familiar with and develop an interest in the community college, they must often be provided with a promising and nonthreatening means of transition into the college environment. The small and rural community colleges responding to the survey often described their programs of transition for both the traditional and the nontraditional student. For example, most reporting community colleges continue to place substantial emphasis upon the traditional high school population. They maintain a constant dialogue with high school teachers, counselors, and administrators, an effort sometimes more effectively accomplished in a rural as opposed to an urban setting. A few of the reporting colleges have developed teacher exchange programs with area high schools, with one having developed a unique high school liaison for college counselors who teach a one-unit college credit class in career guidance to high school juniors. Other measures for assuring high school to community college transition were also reported, including a post-high-school career planning program and a free, two-week skills seminar prior to enrollment in college. Steadily growing in popularity is the two-plus-two concept of establishing a clear and specific link between high school and community college programs, and the practice of "early admission" into college credit courses for qualified high school students while they remain enrolled in high school. In at least one state the simultaneous granting of high school and college credit for honors-level high school courses is now possible.

However, one must not presume that the nontraditional student is being neglected. The homemaker and the senior citizen, the handicapped and the disadvantaged, the displaced American worker and the displaced citizen of a foreign land continue to be central to the mission of all community colleges. In responding to their own specific service areas, the small and rural community colleges are providing basic education for thousands of adults through ESL, ABE, and GED programs. Sometimes by sharing these programs with the public schools, the rural community college is most likely to shoulder the sole responsibility for such opportunity in its service area. Rare in the survey was the community college reporting little or no responsibility for the basic education of adults. In addition, many have specifically addressed economic hardship in their service areas with programs designed to retrain displaced workers. Some of these have worked through JTPA projects or with state agencies to identify those adults needing assistance and to provide transition for them into the college setting for retraining.

ADMISSION

Once the rural community college has gained the interest of a prospective student, it does not diminish its efforts to assist the student in actually entering the community college environment. Many of the colleges reporting in the survey have made the admissions process easy and inviting; most of the others are striving to meet that goal. Counseling is readily available, often months in advance of actual registration and often at off-campus sites most convenient to the service population. Toll-free telephone numbers for information on registration are available at a few of the reporting colleges, and registration by mail and/or phone is becoming much more common. Outreach counselors who field preadmissions problems are becoming more numerous, especially for handicapped and disadvantaged minority students.

Practically every reporting college attempts to assure access by some form of financial assistance. All strive for the lowest possible tuition and fees; all make some form of financial aid available through scholarships, grants, loans, work-study, etc. For convenience, an increasing number of small and rural community colleges are accepting bank card payments for tuition and fees. Many have found the provision of short-term loans to be one of the most successful aids to the student with marginal financial support, and the availability of free child care also appears prominently as a successful aid to student access.

In addition, the small and rural community colleges offer the prospective student substantial assistance in being able to attend classes. Many of the rural community colleges have one or more satellite centers convenient to specific parts of their service areas, with the local shopping center becoming more and more useful for such a purpose. Often a comprehensive array of courses is offered at these centers, but even when the centers are not comprehensive, they reduce the strain on members of the service population of attending class at great distances from home. Several of the colleges reported in the survey that courses are offered at industrial sites, especially when industry-specific training programs have been devised. More than 90 percent of the reporting colleges offer evening classes, and a growing number have instituted weekend colleges for the greater convenience of the service population. Other innovations include open laboratories, which allow moderate to extensive flexibility in the completion of laboratory assignments, and the steady evolution of televised instruction.

PROGRESS

But access, even supported by successful recruiting, varied methods for facilitating student admission, and unique delivery, can not alone assure progress for the student. Based on the survey, small and rural community colleges have come to discover, as have most other community colleges, that special attention must be given to the student after admission and throughout his or her period of study at the college. For a majority of the reporting colleges, that attention begins with a well-developed program of advisement, with some of the most successful programs making extensive use of a system of faculty advisement. A unique system employed by one community college wholly decentralizes counseling and advising by assigning counselors permanently to specific instructional divisions. As would be expected, all of the reporting colleges engage in career and personal counseling to some degree.

A majority of the reporting colleges indicated the use of student orientation activities. For some, those activities are brief and held during registration periods; for others the orientation activities are more elaborate (especially at some residential colleges) and require as much as a full-day program. Several schools described the use of newcomers clubs or organizations, which seem to function in the same manner as parallel community organizations usually sponsored by the chamber of commerce. Some of the small and rural community colleges offer orientation courses for credit that may be either optional or required.

The vast majority of colleges reported participation in a program of assessment, with many using or planning to use mandatory placement. Most of the programs concentrate on assessment of student ability in reading, writing, and mathematics, although some give formal assessments of study skills as well. Actual enrollment in developmental courses at two responding colleges ranged from a low of only 5 percent of the total student body to a high of almost 60 percent. The developmental programs themselves are varied but usually define "levels" of ability through which students must progress. At some of the small and rural colleges, extremely low assessments of ability require students to enroll in a block of developmental courses, with a clear trend toward assuring the student's opportunity for success in college-level work before allowing the student to enter the traditional college-level classes. The rationale for this trend is summarized in the following statement from the catalog of one college:

> By definition, an open-door policy should not imply open access to all programs of the institution. Open access must mean entrance to the institution with restrictions placed on entry into program areas until scholastic skills required for success in those programs have been developed. Some individuals argue against

the philosophy of forced remediation, stating that students entering college have a right to fail. However, we believe that a student has a right to fail only if he/she possesses the scholastic skills necessary to succeed.

An effort to assure that a student "possesses the scholastic skills necessary to succeed" is clearly a goal for all of the colleges reporting in the survey. And new strategies are being pursued to support the student along his or her way to the completion of study. The employment of a retention officer is one strategy reported, while the development of a method of early-warning advisement is another. Most of the reporting schools have established learning assistance centers where students may seek peer or professional tutoring. These centers range from simple writing laboratories to more comprehensive facilities that not only serve the campus community but provide outreach to the community at large. At least six of the reporting colleges claimed the development of learning assistance centers at off-campus sites. Drop-out/stop-out and absentee follow-ups were widely reported as many colleges move toward more elaborate schemes of tracking students and verifying student success. In every case there is a commitment to assure opportunity for progress after access.

EDUCATIONAL OPPORTUNITY

There are of course no astounding results from the survey, no major breakthroughs, no evidence of panacea. What is clearly evident, however, is an ongoing commitment to attract and permit entry into expanded educational opportunity for all individuals who desire that opportunity. It is the traditional commitment of the community college. But at one with that commitment is also a determination to assure adequate preparation for opportunity: to be honest. in assessment but compassionate in providing support and, when necessary, remediation for progress. In spite of their diversity in location, size, and service population, the small and rural community colleges in America demonstrate the above commitment, and in so doing they reflect the best attributes of all American community colleges.

John E. Pickelman is president of Galveston College in Galveston, Texas.

Marc A. Nigliazzo is vice president and dean of Galveston College.

Commission on Small and/or Rural Community Colleges
American Association of Community and Junior Colleges
July 1, 1987–June 30, 1988
(Year Terms Expire in Parentheses)

Donald J. Donato, Chair   (1989)
President
Niagara County Community College
Sanborn, New York

Anthony Calabro   (1990)
President
Western Nevada Community College
Carson City, Nevada

Catherine P. Cornelius   (1990)
President
South Florida Community College
Avon Park, Florida

Kent Farnsworth   (1989)
President
Crowder College
Neosho, Missouri

Gerald H. Fisher (1988)
President
Garland County Community College
Hot Springs, Arkansas

Judson H. Flower (1989)
President
Miles Community College
Miles City, Montana

Kermit Lidstrom (1988)
President
Bismarck Junior College
Bismarck, North Dakota

John E. Pickelman (1990)
President
Galveston College
Galveston, Texas

Robert C. Schleiger (1988)
President
Chesapeake College
Wye Mills, Maryland

Billy B. Thames (1989)
President
Copiah-Lincoln Junior College
Wesson, Mississippi

Marvin L. Vasher (1990)
President
Northland Pioneer College
Holbrook, Arizona

Harold Wade (1988)
President
Walker State Technical College
Sumiton, Alabama

D. Kent Sharples
(Board Liaison)
President
Horry-Georgetown Technical College
Conway, South Carolina